More Praise for *The Core*

"Simple, biblical, and elegant. Invest in your people who, in turn, invest in your customers who, in turn, invest in your business."

—Joe Slawek, chairman and CEO of FONA International Inc. (retired)

"*The Core* is a timely reminder that real leadership is built from the inside out, grounded in character, conviction, and a genuine commitment to serve others. In a season where authentic leadership is increasingly rare, Dr. Paden and Dr. Jones offer an essential guide for leaders who are committed to leading with integrity, humility, and courage."

—Marcylle Combs, owner of MAC Legacy

"Dr. Ken Jones is a man of principle. For more than twenty years as one of his mentors, I have come to know him and the principles he teaches are the basis of his deep wisdom. The principles in this book are some of his very best. Build on them with confidence in your leadership journey."

—Bobb Biehl, executive mentor

"If your character is flawed, influence is forfeited. At last, a leadership book that dares to connect biblical truth with modern business. Jones and Paden give a practical game plan for integrating life and leadership. Read *The Core*. . . . It will help you become a leader worth following!"

—Randy Gravitt, CEO of Lead Every Day and author of *Winning Begins at Home*

"Insightful. Impactful. Indispensable. *The Core* belongs on every leader's desk—regardless of title or industry."

—Cicely Simpson, founder and CEO of 21st Century Leadership Institute and bestselling author

"Dr. Paden writes with the kind of wisdom that only comes from experience. This book is thoughtful, grounded, deeply practical, and a rare leadership guide that speaks as clearly to the heart as it does to the realities of running an organization."

—Lisa Piercey, MD, MBA, managing partner of Tristela Capital Partners

"For anyone who's ever led from a place of exhaustion or discouragement, *The Core* is a lifeline to help you lead well."

—Dr. Kathy Crockett, executive coach, speaker, professor, and corporate leadership development programmer

"Our leadership team had the privilege of sitting under Dr. Jones's teachings. He is a remarkable mentor who reshaped the way we view influence and service in leadership. In his new book, *The Core*, Dr. Jones distills decades of wisdom into practical, deep-rooted principles. We are thankful for his humility and courage in sharing his wisdom with the world."

—Holly Hope, founder of Betenbough Companies

"I am confident that those who read this book and apply the eight core principles will walk away inspired and better prepared to lead in their families, organizations, and communities."

—Rodney Cates, chief human resources officer of Madera Companies

"It is refreshing to read a real leadership book that reflects the values and leadership journeys of its authors. Not a book that says *Do what I say* or *write* but one that shows *This is what I strive to practice every day*."

—Dr. Ray Eldridge, dean emeritus and professor of Management College of Business at Lipscomb University, Lieutenant Colonel US Army (Retired)

"As a leader, I'm always looking for smart resources that will help me serve the people I care about most even better. This is one of them! *The Core* reminds us that leadership isn't about climbing ladders but about building people. It's timeless wisdom for anyone who wants to lead with strength and heart."

—Jon Acuff, New York Times bestselling author of
Soundtracks: The Surprising Solution to Overthinking

"A leader must remember: It's not enough to know. *The Core* is a how to book scaffolded in practicality and anchored in scripture, the tentacles of which make these time-tested principles impossible to forget."

—Sherri Coale, bestselling author, speaker, consultant,
and Hall of Fame women's basketball coach

"In *The Core*, Paden and Jones masterfully bridge ancient biblical wisdom and modern leadership challenges. As someone who serves both in the courtroom and the classroom, I've seen these eight principles transform leaders across generations. Whether you're leading a Fortune 500 company, a church, or a family, this book will recalibrate your understanding of what it means to truly work for the good of your people."

—Mark Lanier, author and founder of
Lanier Law Firm and Lanier Theological Library

"*The Core* is an excellent leadership book built on eight basic principles that apply to just about every leadership role. Review the titles for each of the eight chapters, and you will be sold, and once you start reading, you will have a hard time putting the book down."

—Joe Scarlett, chairman and CEO of
Tractor Supply Company (retired)

"At a moment when strong, values-based leadership is in short supply, *The Core* delivers clarity, conviction, and practical guidance. Jones and Paden offer eight essential principles that cut through today's chaos and complexity. Their message is leadership isn't about titles or positions—it's about influence, service, and character. The Core will challenge you, equip you, and inspire you to lead with authenticity in every sphere of life."

—Dee Ann Turner, bestselling author, international speaker,
and vice president of Chick-fil-A (retired)

THE CORE

THE CORE

8 Principles for Building Strong, Authentic Leadership

BY DR. MATT PADEN WITH DR. L. KEN JONES

Forefront
BOOKS

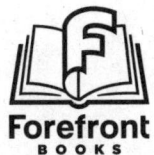

The Core: 8 Principles for Building Strong, Authentic Leadership
Copyright © 2026 by Matt Paden and L. Ken Jones

All rights reserved. No part of this publication may be reproduced, stored in a retrieval system, or transmitted in any form by any means, electronic, mechanical, photocopy, recording, or otherwise, without the prior permission of the publisher, except as provided by USA copyright law.

No patent liability is assumed with respect to the use of the information contained herein. Although every precaution has been taken in the preparation of this book, the publisher and author assume no responsibility for errors or omissions. Neither is any liability assumed for damages resulting from the use of the information contained herein.

This book is intended for informational purposes only. It is not intended to be used as the sole basis for financial or investing decisions, nor should it be construed as advice designed to meet the particular needs of an individual's situation.

Unless otherwise indicated, Scripture quotations are from the Holy Bible, New International Version®, NIV®, Copyright © 1973, 1978, 1984, 2011 by Biblica, Inc.™ Used by permission of Zondervan. All rights reserved worldwide.

Scripture quotations marked ESV are from the ESV® Bible (The Holy Bible, English Standard Version®), copyright ©2001 by Crossway, a publishing ministry of Good News Publishers. Used by permission. All rights reserved.

Scripture quotations marked KJV are from the King James Version. Public domain.

Scripture quotations marked MSG are taken from THE MESSAGE, copyright © 1993, 2002, 2018 by Eugene H. Peterson. Used by permission of NavPress, represented by Tyndale House Publishers. All rights reserved.

Published by Forefront Books, Nashville, Tennessee.
Distributed by Simon & Schuster.

Library of Congress Control Number: 2026900132

Print ISBN: 978-1-63763-558-2
E-book ISBN: 978-1-63763-559-9

Cover Design by Michelle Manley
Interior Design by PerfecType, Nashville, TN

Printed in the United States of America.

26 27 28 29 30 31 RR4 10 9 8 7 6 5 4 3 2 1

Dr. L. Ken Jones' Dedication for the Book

How does one dedicate a book that contains the core of one of my life's major passions - leadership? Long ago, I wrote my personal mission statement, "To be a teacher for the improvement of life according to the design and will of God". The study of leadership was one of the pathways to fulfill this mission or purpose.

So, to all who have taught me by their lectures, books and examples, I dedicate this book. To all who have worked with me through the years to help me lead and learn to lead, I dedicate this book. To my wife, Suzie, who has walked beside me on life's journey, I dedicate this book. And to my God and Lord Jesus, who gave me grace, salvation and scripture, which teaches leadership better than any other, I dedicate this book.

Dr. Matt Paden's Dedication for the Book

For most of my adult life, I have talked about the books I wanted to write. The number of book outlines with catchy titles sitting on my laptop is greater than I care to admit. I would have never moved from those dreams to this reality without the encouragement, love, and support of my wife, Kagney, and our kids, Zaylee and Parker. You three inspire me daily to live out my purpose, trust in the Lord, and make sure my words and actions align. For all of this and so much more, I dedicate this book to you.

CONTENTS

FOREWORD	Dr. John Delony	13
INTRODUCTION	Dr. L. Ken Jones	19
INTRODUCTION	Dr. Matt Paden	25

Part 1: For the Good of the People

CHAPTER 1	The Retirement Dinner	33
CHAPTER 2	A Summer Internship	37
CHAPTER 3	The Visitation	43
CHAPTER 4	May I Tell You a Story?	49
CHAPTER 5	A Queen, an Egomaniac, and a Guy Named Mordecai	53
CHAPTER 6	If I Perish, I Perish	61
CHAPTER 7	The Coach and the Fog	65
CHAPTER 8	As Good as Our People	73
CHAPTER 9	Two Great Days	79
CHAPTER 10	Truth and Grace	85
CHAPTER 11	A Future Here	93
CHAPTER 12	The Stories That People Tell about You	97
CHAPTER 13	A Farewell Speech	103
CHAPTER 14	The Next Chapter	107

Part 2: The Leadership Core

CHAPTER 15	Work for the Good of the People	115
CHAPTER 16	Keep Your Ego in Check	133
CHAPTER 17	Embrace Truth	141
CHAPTER 18	Lead with Your Ears	151
CHAPTER 19	Show Up with Grace	161
CHAPTER 20	Pace Yourself and Extend the Game	179
CHAPTER 21	Be Coachable	201
CHAPTER 22	Know Where You're Going and Why	213

CONCLUSION	227
ACKNOWLEDGMENTS	231
ABOUT THE AUTHORS	235

FOREWORD

I've known Dr. Ken Jones and Dr. Matt Paden for almost thirty years. It is surreal to type this—few people get to have thirty-year relationships with anyone, much less with two men of high character both in their forward-facing roles and behind closed doors, with their spouses, their kids, their friends, and their faith communities.

I met Dr. Ken Jones when I was an arrogant, loud-mouthed eighteen-year-old. Dr. Jones was the president of a small, faith-based university, and I showed up to his campus looking for trouble. In reflection, I was little more than a scared kid, having just moved nine hours away from everything and everyone I knew, far from the trees and rain and big city where I grew up, to the endless sunsets, treeless cottonfields, and slower-paced community of West Texas. I entered most rooms with a cocktail of bravado, opinion, and Texas-sized ego, trying to protect myself from the realities of early-adulthood fears and insecurities. I was a whirling dervish—or as my wife once told me, "I was a lot."

Even through my late teenage chaos, I could see—and more importantly feel—that public-facing Dr. Jones was a strong, rooted presence. He was different from any suit I'd ever encountered. He commanded my respect not because he was bombastic or loud but because when he spoke, I knew he respected and cared for me and my fellow students first. He listened intently and believed the words he spoke. Dr. Jones was a captivating public speaker, a deep thinker with iron-clad integrity, and the first academic I'd ever met who also preached and ran cattle on the weekends. In a twist of fate, I also got to know Ken as the father of one of my new college friends. I got behind-the-curtains insight into how the man on the stage also loved and honored his family and his church. I don't know a lot of eighteen-year-olds who talk with unwavering respect and love for their dad—but Ken's son did.

Dr. Ken Jones spent his career studying leadership both academically and theologically, and he always took the lessons out of the classroom and into the real world. He didn't just drop academic jargon and platitudes about God—he believed them. And more importantly, he lived them. I ended my college career as the student body president, giving me a ringside seat to watch a man of character listen, learn, and live the life of a servant-focused, Godly leader. Years later, Dr. Jones gave me my first job as a university leader, which ultimately changed my family's life. We worked side by side, and he became one of my first and most important mentors, teaching me to channel my confusion, energy, and ego into values-based service, humility, strength, and integrity. My children have a different life because Dr. Jones invested in me.

I met Dr. Matt Paden just a few years after I met Dr. Jones, but in a completely different context. I met Matt in the dorm. We were college students together, figuring out how to do laundry, get to class on time, and grow up to be men of character. I was a few years older than Matt, but even when he was a teenager, I recognized his leadership, both behind closed doors and beyond. He was a member of our university basketball team, where he commanded the respect of his coaches and teammates. He was honorable and principled, even at nineteen, when most of us were not. Matt was a young man who always did the next right thing and ultimately also found his way into university leadership. While I was off studying psychology and counseling, Dr. Paden dug into the literature on individual and organizational leadership. He has always been keenly interested in what makes a good leader and, more importantly, how good leaders lead in the real world. He's led large teams, taught graduate leadership courses, and developed and walked alongside leaders at the world's largest companies. More impressively, he's maintained leadership roles in his local church, kept his entrepreneurial edge with his own projects, and never forgotten where leadership matters most: in his home. The highest compliment I can pay Dr. Paden is that he is a world-class husband and father. He is also my great friend.

In a world where it seems everyone with a podcast or AI prompt is throwing leadership advice around like confetti, Dr. Paden has developed the rarest of qualities: a deep understanding of the scientific literature, an extraordinary ability to communicate wisdom in a digestible way, and his own leadership scars from years of leading large and small teams of his own.

For the past twenty-five years, Dr. Paden and I have risen through the ranks of leadership together, often across the country from each other, but always a phone call away. I was always wheeling and dealing, and he was a steady presence, always thoughtful, strong, and service minded. And like me, he was deeply impacted by the opportunity to work alongside and be mentored by Dr. Jones.

Together, they have written what I consider to be an exceedingly important book for our day and age.

At the macro level, over the past three decades I've grown disheartened as leadership in our homes, our churches, our businesses, and even in our country has deteriorated beyond recognition. Leadership has often become all about the leader: their ego, their compensation plan, their desires, and ultimately what they can get from the people who work "under them." Leadership has become about personalities, being loud, unpredictable, and egocentric. It's hard to know who to trust, who has hard-earned wisdom underneath their ideas, and who can take ancient wisdom and align it with the transforming nature of modern families, businesses, churches, and government. Countless times I've wished that someone would take the lessons I learned from Dr. Jones, and with Dr. Paden, and compile them for those who are sick of the leaders who are running our world into the ground. The world feels as though it is being remade in real time, and there seem to be fewer and fewer trustworthy leaders to turn to. I have been privileged over the years to have Dr. Paden's and Dr. Jones's cell phone numbers when I needed support. Now you have access to their wisdom too.

In *The Core: 8 Principles for Building Strong, Authentic Leadership*, Dr. Paden and Dr. Jones have taken their decades of leadership wisdom and distilled it into a strong foundation for true leadership—one based not on whims and platitudes but on biblical wisdom, scholarship, and real-world experience. Thank God.

In *The Core*, the authors brilliantly weave foundational leadership principles through both story and practical framework, allowing the reader to experience leadership through the lens of a mentor-mentee relationship and walk away with concrete tools for building their own leadership foundation. While most leadership writers either use some sort of autobiographical narrative to try to generalize leadership principles or simply dump a load of academic big words and charts and tables on an already-overwhelmed reader, Paden and Jones do something different. They use a fictional story to explore the reflection of a retiring senior leader and his decades-long mentorship. Through the use of story, the authors help us feel the lessons before they articulate them, bringing them from the page and into our hearts.

The book then transitions to a grounded, timeless framework, one that any leader at any age or stage can use to reflect on their own leadership and reimagine how and why they lead. While most leadership books are merely a compilation of tips, tricks, and hacks, *The Core* takes us back to ourselves, the man or woman in the mirror, and walks us through the challenging process of honest reflection and the truths about leadership: Leaders exist for others, not for themselves. Leadership is about people before balance sheets, integrity before being always right, and about humility and service before corner offices and pride. *The Core* is a clarion call for leaders to return to their rightful place underneath organizations, not on top of them. This work holds the leader accountable to who and why they are leading in the first place, and where they want to take those in their care. Extraordinary leaders listen more than they speak, they work to see and know those they are leading, they take care of themselves, and they are powered by a deep and resonating "why." Drs. Paden and Jones show you why this matters, and how to do it.

I consider some of the most prolific leadership writers—including Dave Ramsey, Dr. Henry Cloud, Pat Lencioni, and John

Maxwell—good friends. I've also personally been inspired by leadership writers like Dr. Angela Duckworth, Simon Sinek, Susan Cain, Dr. Brené Brown, and Jocko Willink. Dr. Paden and Dr. Jones have written a book that belongs right alongside these greats, on the desk and in the bag of every leader.

It's been one of my life's great honors to lead with and alongside Dr. Ken Jones and Dr. Matt Paden. I've been inspired by their tenacity, humility, and desire to take risks on behalf of those they love and those they are leading. I have learned powerful lessons on how to lead, love, and do life well.

In a loud, obnoxious, clickbaity world gone mad, many leaders are considering quitting. Few leaders have inner strength, a rooted sense of purpose, and the skills to show up as a calm, strong presence when everything feels likes it's on fire.

You can transform your leadership.

You can reimagine what it means to lead and then begin, from the inside out, to become the leader the world is crying out for you to become.

We need you to lead, and to lead well.

This book shows you how.

Dr. John Delony, bestselling author
and host of the *Dr. John Delony Show*

MY LEADERSHIP JOURNEY

Often I have heard people use the term *core*. Having served as president of two universities combined for over two decades, I have listened to many discussions about the "core curriculum"—a block of courses that each student is required to take in order to earn a bachelor's degree.

The core curriculum generally includes basic cornerstone courses, such as English, history, math, and science. The rationale behind this curriculum is that if every student took a common set of classes, individual disciplines could then add other specially designed courses on top of the "core," thus properly training students in a chosen academic discipline.

A second way I've heard the term *core* used is in regard to physical fitness. Over the years, I have been a member of numerous fitness centers. On occasion, I've sought advice from personal trainers. They often speak of the "core," which is a group of muscles in the torso area. These muscles provide the foundation of the body's strength, and they're responsible for things like balance, stability, and the general ability to adequately handle routine physical demands. If the physical core is being strengthened, other areas of the body are also being strengthened.

These "core" analogies are key to the heart of this book. Multitudes of wonderful theories, teachings, and assessments related to leadership exist in our world. Leadership books, podcasts, speeches, seminars, and training manuals are plentiful in the leadership landscape. Most of these resources are beneficial tools for leaders. However, this book offers something a little different—the idea that there is a "Leadership Core." And unless that core is strong, studying all the leadership theories in the world may not be enough to allow someone to become a truly effective leader.

For more than forty years, I have been in leadership roles. Almost from the beginning, I became a student of leadership. Scores of leadership books, seminars, consultants, and coaches were all a part of my pursuit of knowledge. But over the years, I've found the greatest leadership resource to be the Bible. I've studied the lives of Moses, Joshua, Deborah, David, Nehemiah, Daniel, Paul, and others. Looking at their lives from the viewpoint of leadership proved to be fertile ground for developing my own leadership skills.

Of course, the greatest teacher and example of leadership is Jesus. Some of you who pick up this book may not appreciate the frequent references to Bible stories, but I encourage you not to skip over those parts. I use these stories and examples not to try to persuade you about biblical belief but rather because, in my opinion, the Bible is the best leadership resource I have ever found.

In addition to studying leadership, I have tried to intentionally put the lessons I have learned into practice as part of everyday life. As an educator and speaker, I know there is a difference between "knowing" and "doing." One Bible writer urges us not just to hear what to do but to do what we hear: "Do not merely listen to the word, and so deceive yourselves. Do what it says" (James 1:22).

So, here I am—almost forty years later. The big question for me after all of this, is: *What do I know about leadership?*

In June of 2012, I had the opportunity to begin answering that question when I stepped away from a nineteen-year career as president of Lubbock Christian University. The trustees of the university had asked me to take on a new role of chancellor, primarily devoting my time to speaking, teaching, and writing. In this new role, I had the opportunity to reflect on all I'd learned about leadership during my career, identifying the principles I'd been practicing routinely throughout the years.

What I discovered was a bit shocking, at least to me. First, I found that the list of principles I knew and used routinely was not very long and didn't have a great deal to do with the "skills" so often associated with leadership. Second, I noticed that what was on the list was actually very simple to understand. Finally, I realized that while the principles were few and easy to understand, they were also extremely difficult to consistently put into practice.

After two years of refining and teaching these leadership principles, I condensed forty years of study and practice into what I call the Core of Leadership. Like the fitness analogy, it is this core that allows leaders to be strong, balanced, and effective. And like the university core curriculum, it's what all other theories, skills, and ideas of leadership must be built upon. My belief is that if you don't get the core right, your leadership will not be as effective as it could be.

The ultimate purpose of this book is to teach you the Core of Leadership, giving you a strong foundation to build upon. Our desire is for you to become a tremendous leader. And it starts with a strong core.

Despite all the resources we have available on the topic of leadership, our world still greatly lacks good leaders. In politics, churches, businesses, families, and just about every area of life, good leadership is absent. It doesn't take one long to realize a world without true, others-focused leadership is destined for challenge. Thus, our hope is to change the world by changing the focus of leadership. We aim to deliver the Core of Leadership material in a simple way that allows you to continue learning about and building on that core.

We've designed this book in two parts. In the first part, you will read a fictional story about a man named Clint Smith and his mentor, Dr. Bill Jackson. Dr. Jackson's intentional coaching and mentoring help equip Clint with the strong Core necessary to maximize Clint's natural strengths and gifts. Throughout this narrative, Dr. Jackson guides Clint through a process of redefining what it means to lead people and develop followers.

In part two, you will find a more traditional set of chapters dedicated to better describing the Core of Leadership principles we believe are imperative to becoming a strong and balanced leader. Each chapter will cover one of the eight Core principles in detail:

1. Work for the good of the people.
2. Keep your ego in check.
3. Embrace truth.
4. Lead with your ears.
5. Show up with grace.
6. Pace yourself and extend the game.

7. Be coachable.
8. Know where you're going and why.

Remember, there are many components of leadership, including some good and helpful principles, that this book will not address. That's okay. Other resources cover those topics, and this book is designed to focus on the Core of Leadership. This is important because if the core is not right, nothing will be right.

Please enjoy the leadership journey you're about to take. May God bless you as you grow, learn, and make a positive difference in your world, leading others while you become the leader you were created to be.

Dr L. Ken Jones

A LEADERSHIP MASTERCLASS

As soon as I set foot in the president's office, I was greeted by a frazzled and anxious executive assistant. She hurried me to the waiting area outside the meeting room, where I heard voices engaged in a tense discussion behind the thick wall. The executive assistant said in a hushed tone, "Dr. Jones might need to cancel the trip."

I felt a sting of disappointment. I'd been looking forward to our road trip to Midland, Texas, an oil patch city about two hours south of where I lived in Lubbock, Texas. We were scheduled to have dinner with a small group of loyal alumni and donors, casting vision for the future of our university and asking for their input. Whatever was going on must have been serious to put such an important event in jeopardy.

"Would you mind asking Dr. Jones if I should wait, or if he wants to call it off?" I requested.

The executive assistant looked at me with a deer-in-the-headlights expression on her face. Understandably, she was uncomfortable interrupting the president's meeting, which appeared to be extremely serious. But she knocked, quickly stuck her head into the tense room, and had an answer in just a few seconds: I was to wait until the president's current meeting was finished.

As I settled into a chair in the lobby, my mind raced. What was going on behind that imposing door? A major project on campus had recently reached a critical point after some poor management decisions. Was that the topic of discussion? If so, I knew I would be in for a quiet car ride with the president.

Typically, my car rides with Dr. Jones were filled with conversation. I never missed the opportunity to take advantage of this valuable one-on-one time with the president and CEO of my university, asking him questions, absorbing every ounce of wisdom he shared. A young, aspiring leader who often found himself in the room with more established leaders, I was always hungry to grow. In that season, I was pursuing a doctorate in organizational leadership, reading every leadership book I could get my hands on and listening to lectures by some of the foremost experts on leadership in the world.

But I found that the best learning came from real-life human experiences—observing gifted leaders in meetings, sharing a meal with leaders I admired, or, in this case, taking a road trip together.

Dr. Jones was—and continues to be—one of the most impactful leaders I have ever known. A longtime student of leadership, he communicated leadership lessons with eloquence and depth, especially on the topic of leading like Jesus. Even better? He truly lived it.

My favorite lessons from Dr. Jones came during our car rides as we traveled to conduct university business. Driving through the dry and dusty plains of West Texas and Eastern New Mexico, I received my own masterclass in leadership, better than most leadership presentations I've ever heard.

After this meeting, however, that masterclass would be cancelled—even if the trip wasn't. I would tone down my question-asking and give Dr. Jones some space.

Two minutes after settling into my chair in the lobby, Dr. Jones's office door swung open and one of the key members of his leadership team walked out. My suspicions were confirmed—Dr. Jones had been meeting with the lead on the very project I'd been worried about. I had never seen this man, normally composed and confident, looking so upset. It almost seemed like he'd been crying.

As the man walked right past me without saying anything, a lump formed in my throat. I knew this man was loyal, good, and respected. I felt for him.

From behind me, I heard a voice: "Let's go."

I turned to see Dr. Jones standing in the doorway. He also looked emotional. I grabbed my briefcase and hurried to catch up, as Dr. Jones was already headed to his car. Curious and a bit on edge, my mind was racing with a dozen questions to ask. But I reminded myself I was a mid-level leader, and this situation was likely beyond my "need to know" status.

As we pulled out of the parking lot, I settled in for a long and quiet drive to Midland. Wanting to address the elephant in the car, I said, "There seems to be a lot going on. I appreciate you keeping this event on your schedule. I understand if you need some peace and quiet as we drive."

Dr. Jones nodded, a strained look on his face. He appeared to have heard me, but clearly his mind was far away.

We hadn't traveled two blocks from campus when Dr. Jones broke the silence and said, "Matt, leadership is really hard. But we must always face the truth head-on and do what is right."

I sat quietly, unsure whether I should respond or wait for him to say more.

There was, in fact, more. On that drive, I had one of the most meaningful conversations I've ever been a part of. Not just about leadership but about life. Dr. Jones shared some of his deepest personal reflections. He spoke about empowering and trusting team members, even when they make mistakes. He talked about the importance of embracing truth, about offering grace while still holding people accountable for their words and actions.

Knowing I had just witnessed a key leader walk out of that meeting, Dr. Jones directly addressed my curiosity: "He resigned today and will be leaving the university." He then shared the facts without ever speaking poorly of the man, refusing to let his emotions drive his behavior. In fact, he relayed multiple stories about the good work this leader had done for the university community over the years.

Watching Dr. Jones process this challenging development in real time was riveting. He did not minimize the complexity and difficulty of the situation, yet he remained steady, staying focused on the big picture and the mission he had been called to complete. Not once did he make it about himself. His words left no doubt in my mind that a leader can work for the good of the people they are entrusted to lead but also stay strong, hold others accountable for their actions, and effectively deal with the messes that inevitably arise.

We arrived at the dinner just in time. As we gathered our belongings and headed toward the front door, I walked behind Dr. Jones, thinking, *This is the kind of leader I want to follow. This is the kind of leader I want to be.*

• • •

This book is full of principles and lessons, many of which I—and so many others—have learned from Dr. Jones. It is rich, human, and brimming with not just knowledge but wisdom from lived experience. We desperately need more leaders like Dr. Jones—men and women who work for the good of the people, aren't afraid of truth, and steward the mission entrusted to them.

We live in a world full of chaos, noise, hurt, and despair. Our modern environment is full of blessings and conveniences. Yet it also brings complexity, anxiety, and challenges we've never encountered before. In a critical moment, good leaders are in short supply. Our culture is full of aspiring leaders, but they're given poor, narcissistic models, while living overcommitted, exhausted lives. And they either fail to find their stride or lack the depth to truly make an impact.

My coauthor and I feel a call to raise up the next generation of leaders. We want to share some of the principles and lessons we've learned as lifelong students of leadership. These lessons weren't learned in a classroom but through real-life, hands-on experiences—often terrifying, usually exhilarating, always instructive.

We've led teams and worked with leaders and organizations for decades. And we continue to study leadership because we believe it is mandatory to move our communities, churches, organizations, and families from where they are currently to where they should be.

We also believe that leadership is for *everyone*. It's not just for CEOs, presidents, business executives, coaches, politicians, and community organizers. Nor is leadership limited to a set of skills to be developed by the rich, powerful, or highly educated.

Leadership is for the retired individual and the new graduate, the stay-at-home parent and the working professional, the introvert and the extrovert, the employee of a large organization and the freelancer who works from home—and everyone in between. It's for the teenagers in our church youth groups, the college students who inhabit our campuses, the hippies and the hipsters, the Boomers and the Millennials, Gen X, Gen Z and Gen Alpha, and everyone who calls this planet home.

All of us need to be reminded we have what it takes to lead. Dr. Jones did that for me. At his encouragement, I studied leadership at the doctoral level. His influence charted the course of my life, as I now spend my days coaching, encouraging, and developing leaders. Even though our professional lives have taken us to different parts of the country, Dr. Jones's mentoring has continued from a distance. He is always willing to answer a phone call or a text, or even arrange a personal visit, to help me through a leadership "opportunity" (my word for *challenge*) that has reared its ugly head. And I still feel as humble and grateful as I did on those car rides long ago.

It is virtually impossible to separate the study of leadership from the study of life and personal growth, especially spiritual growth. The life-changing idea of the leadership Core, as outlined in this book, will transform how you lead your teams, organizations, families, and community. My hope is that by leading well, you will inspire and motivate others to do so as well, and the ripple effect will make a difference throughout the world.

Dr. Matt Paden

For the Good of the People

1. The Retirement Dinner
2. A Summer Internship
3. The Visitation
4. May I Tell You a Story?
5. A Queen, an Egomaniac, and a Guy Named Mordecai
6. If I Perish, I Perish
7. The Coach and the Fog
8. As Good as Our People
9. Two Great Days
10. Truth and Grace
11. A Future Here
12. The Stories That People Tell about You
13. A Farewell Speech
14. The Next Chapter

CHAPTER 1

The Retirement Dinner

Clint Smith sat at a round table for eight in the back half of a large ballroom, taking in the moment. Even though he had known this day was coming for over a year, he still wasn't ready for it. Tonight was a celebration, but Clint found himself feeling a bit overwhelmed and somewhat emotional as the evening began.

For the past fifteen months or so, Clint and his coworkers had been preparing themselves for the retirement of Dr. Bill Jackson, the longtime CEO of Grace Harbor Regional Hospital. In his nearly thirty-year run, Dr. Jackson had led Grace Harbor through a season of unprecedented success, growth, and stability.

The hospital had more than doubled its overall impact on the community, no matter which set of metrics you looked at. As important as it had been to stabilize Grace Harbor's financial and business operations, it had been just as important for Dr. Jackson to improve the hospital's reputation in the community as an industry leader, not a second-rate place to receive medical care.

When Jackson had arrived at Grace Harbor decades earlier, he had no idea that local politicians and community leaders—many of whom were now in this ballroom—had been having secret meetings among themselves to discuss what could be done with the hospital facilities, land, and infrastructure should Grace Harbor's dire financial situation continue to deteriorate.

The hospital didn't end up closing, as the negative predictions had once suggested, and Dr. Jackson was leaving Grace Harbor in much better condition than it had been in when he'd first arrived. Over the last few weeks, the conversation around town had centered on the positive changes Dr. Jackson had helped the hospital make during his tenure.

But a shadow was cast over the day's festivities. Many were voicing doubts that the next CEO would be capable of filling Dr. Jackson's shoes. The hospital and its community of doctors, nurses, staff members, board members, volunteers, and donors would miss the retiring CEO greatly.

Most of all, Clint Smith would miss him.

If Dr. Jackson had had his way, there would be no party in his honor. But his team and his community insisted on the celebration. He had meant too much to them, and they felt he deserved to be honored at a series of events throughout the year where various groups could tell him, "Thank you." This was to be the last of those events, the largest and most public and, according to Dr. Jackson, the one he was most ready to have behind him.

THE RETIREMENT DINNER

Across the room from Clint, Dr. Jackson sat at the head table and picked at his food. He knew he would be asked to say a few words at the end of the evening, and he was now second-guessing the speech he'd planned.

His wife, June, saw him fidgeting with his food and looking at the notecards on his lap under the table. She had seen him give hundreds—if not thousands—of speeches before, so she knew he was displaying a different type of nervous energy. Gently touching his arm, she smiled at him. When he saw her smile, he grinned back and said, "If this is my last speech to this group, I don't want to waste this opportunity."

His wife nodded, looked him in the eye, and said, "Forget your notes—just speak from the core."

He knew immediately what she meant, and it gave him the strength he needed in that moment.

A Summer Internship

Dr. Jackson wasn't the only person at the event without an appetite. Seated in the back of the room, Clint Smith had barely touched his plate. His desire for the "banquet chicken" was waning as the evening went on, and as his wife and the others at the table made conversation, he found himself lost in his own thoughts.

Clint had been a part of the Grace Harbor Community for two decades and was seen as an up-and-coming leader with a bright future in hospital administration. He had grown up in the city where Grace Harbor was located, and he had enough memories as a longtime citizen of the community, combined with institutional knowledge gained from working at the hospital, to know that this leadership transition was significant.

Clint hadn't planned on working in hospital administration, let alone ever considered returning to his hometown to start his career. His original plan was to play college football, then move to Dallas or

Houston and land a job in big finance or with a consulting company connected to the alumni boosters who supported his college football team. Always competitive, he'd had his sights set on working his way into a fancy corner office in a downtown high-rise.

He had lofty dreams and goals—and the talent to go with them. Most of the people in his hometown were just as surprised as Clint was when he found himself back in town after college, his once-promising football career having ended prematurely at the end of his junior year.

Clint's first true connection to the work of Grace Harbor Regional Hospital had come when he was twenty-one years old, after the first real setback in his rather charmed life. In the late spring of his junior year, he was in a nasty car accident while visiting home. His injuries were not life-threatening, but having both legs and his abdomen seriously injured left him unable to continue playing football.

Emergency responders to the accident weren't sure how he had survived. They rushed Clint to Grace Harbor just a couple of blocks away, where the surgeons and doctors took good care of him in those early hours. Thanks to their exceptional care, he was able to enjoy a fairly normal and active lifestyle all these years later—even though his college football dream had come to a close.

While in the hospital for a few days after the accident, Clint, devastated by the bad news about football but grateful to be alive, received a wide range of visitors. As word spread of his accident, he was visited by family, friends, coaches, teammates, and people from his hometown church. He was also surprised to receive a visit from Dr. Bill Jackson, the CEO of the hospital and—up until now—a total stranger.

Dr. Jackson, who was often in meetings putting out organizational fires or trying to raise money for the next special project, didn't have much time to visit patients in his hospital. But he had heard about the local football star's accident and wanted to swing by and offer some encouragement to the young man.

All these years later, Clint recalled Dr. Jackson asking him about his injuries and the timeline for his rehabilitation and recovery. He also remembered telling the CEO that because of the recuperation process, he'd have to decline a corporate internship he'd had scheduled for that summer. Dr. Jackson briefly encouraged Clint to stay positive, work hard on his recovery, and try and keep things in perspective. The two exchanged a handshake, and Dr. Jackson was gone as quickly as he'd come

A few days later, as Clint's family was packing his things in preparation for his discharge from the hospital, Clint was receiving instructions from the nursing staff . . . when there was a knock on the door. It was Dr. Jackson. The nurses, having seen their executive leader in the room just a few days prior, were a little surprised that he was visiting yet again, but they seemed excited to see him. They finished their immediate tasks and left the room so Dr. Jackson could visit with Clint alone.

Upon entering the room, Dr. Jackson asked, "Clint, do you mind if we talk for just a moment?"

"Sure," Clint responded. "I believe this is your hospital room."

Dr. Jackson laughed and said, "I've been thinking about what you and I talked about a couple of days ago."

Clint, who had spent the past few days taking a significant amount of pain medication and couldn't easily recall most of the conversations he'd had during his time in the hospital, looked at Dr. Jackson with a puzzled expression on his face.

"Clint," Dr. Jackson reminded him, "a couple days ago when I came by to say hello, you mentioned how disappointed you were that your injuries would keep you from playing football again. While I wish I could help you with that, I can't, but I do have an idea how to help you with the other situation you were disappointed about—having to give up your internship. In all my years as the CEO of Grace Harbor, I've never had an intern, but since you'll be in town and spending part of your summer in physical therapy in our facility anyway, would you be interested in being my first official intern this summer? I know you had your heart set on interning for a big corporation, but I think we can offer you a great opportunity. You'll learn everything from finance to marketing to operations to—well, you name it, we do it."

Clint nodded his head as Dr. Jackson continued. "I've heard from many people in this town that you have a lot of leadership potential. A summer interning here at the hospital could help you grow and develop as a leader and prepare you for whatever profession you go into. What do you say? You want to spend the summer helping me work for the good of these fine people at Grace Harbor?"

Clint, who had been so brokenhearted about everything that he hadn't considered any type of plan B, didn't really know how to respond beyond a half-hearted, "Yes."

"Great!" Dr. Jackson grinned. "I look forward to working with you. You can focus on strengthening your core in the early mornings with our wonderful therapists, and we can work on your leadership Core the rest of the day. I'll see you in a couple of weeks."

With that, Dr. Jackson stood up, shook Clint's hand, and exited the room.

Clint, not sure what had just happened, or why he'd be doing core workouts with the CEO, went back to preparing to leave his Grace Harbor Hospital room.

The Visitation

"Why are you grinning like that?" asked Clint's wife, Kristen, interrupting her husband's trip down memory lane.

"Oh, I'm sorry, I got caught up in a reflective moment," Clint said, sitting up straighter in his chair and adjusting the napkin on his lap.

Kristen leaned close and spoke into her husband's ear. "You've been reflecting since we got here. It would be great if you could engage in this table conversation for a little bit."

"Sure, I'm sorry—this is just a lot to take in. Don't worry, I'm good," reassured Clint.

At that moment, Frank Williams, a local business leader sitting at the table with them, said, "Clint, I understand you've spent a lot of time with Dr. Jackson over the years. I'm sure you have some good stories to tell about him."

Clint grinned and said, "Oh, I've got stories, all right."

Frank asked, "What do you think he'll talk about when he gets up to speak?"

Clint didn't have to think twice. "I'm certain he'll talk about the Leadership Core. Oh, and about a guy named Mordecai."

The guests around the table stared at Clint, confused.

"Were you on his speechwriting team for tonight?" someone joked.

"No, I just know how important the topic of leadership is to Dr. Jackson. With this room full of leaders and future leaders, he won't be able to help himself," Clint said. Then he quietly added, "I hope he talks about it one more time."

The dinner conversation switched to another topic. Clint took a deep breath and drank some of his tea, grateful he seemed to be off the hook as the table's resident Dr. Jackson expert.

As the servers began to scurry around the ballroom offering coffee to the guests, Clint forgot his promise to Kristen about staying present in the evening and began to reminisce again.

His mind went back to his first week as an intern in Dr. Bill Jackson's office at Grace Harbor. The office had been nicely appointed and professional but not flashy. It wasn't how the young intern planned on decorating his own office when he one day became a big corporate executive, but it would do for this summer.

Clint had spent the past several weeks in physical therapy, building his strength back up after the accident. His PT sessions were always scheduled for early in the morning, before he reported for duty in the CEO's office. Clint's experience as a strong, competitive athlete was paying off—he was already seeing improvement in his ability to move. While still unable to drive, he was grateful for his family members who woke up early to bring him to therapy and pick him up after he was done interning for the day.

Clint's first few days in the office were spent getting oriented. He met the administrative team, took a facility tour, and learned about the current projects Dr. Jackson and his team were focused on. Dr. Jackson had been out of town at a conference for most of the first week of Clint's internship, and Clint wondered if he would actually get to spend time with his new boss or if this internship would be the "Hey kid, bring us some coffee" kind of arrangement.

On Friday morning, he got his answer.

Dr. Jackson, now back in town, was waiting for Clint to arrive in his office after finishing physical therapy for the day. "Clint," he said when the young man arrived, "I'm so glad you're here. I hope you've had a good week in the office. Let's get in the car."

Clint, surprised at the invitation but eager to get out of the office, grinned and followed Dr. Jackson to the parking lot, where his boss apologized for not having parked in a handicapped spot and offered to push Clint's wheelchair for him. Clint declined, opting for the extra workout and wheeling himself to the car. Surely the CEO's spot would be close to the building.

As the two made their way across the enormous parking lot, Clint realized he'd made a mistake in not accepting the help. Apparently, Dr. Jackson liked to park as far away from the facility as possible. While that didn't seem like "normal" CEO behavior to Clint, he didn't say anything. He was too tired from wheeling his chair across the parking lot.

After Dr. Jackson loaded Clint's wheelchair into the car, Clint settled in, welcoming the air conditioning blasting through the vents. "Dr. Jackson, I'm excited to see what a CEO does. So, where are we going today?" Clint assumed they were headed to a meeting with the mayor or a major donor to the hospital.

Dr. Jackson said, "First, we're going to stop by a funeral home about forty-five miles north of here, and then we'll head over to the university."

Who died? Clint wondered. *It must be someone very important.*

Eyes fixed on the road, Dr. Jackson asked Clint about how his physical therapy was coming along. He seemed genuinely happy to learn it would only be another few weeks before Clint could move from the wheelchair to crutches.

Clint was amazed by how many questions Dr. Jackson asked. After discussing rehab, they talked about Clint's school schedule for the upcoming fall semester and how he was navigating the loss of football in his life. The forty-five-minute car ride seemed over in a matter of minutes. As they pulled into the funeral home parking lot, Clint remembered he still didn't know why they were going there.

Dr. Jackson put the vehicle in park and jumped out of the car to retrieve Clint's wheelchair from the back. He grinned and said, "I suspect you'll let me push you across the parking lot this time?"

Clint grinned back and agreed it might be a good plan.

Before entering the funeral home, Dr. Jackson paused, looked Clint in the eye, and said, "Clint, one of our longtime employees, someone I've worked with ever since I started at Grace Harbor, unexpectedly lost her husband to a heart attack this week. She's a gifted and special person who means a lot to our community. We won't linger here too long, but I do hope to spend some time talking and praying with her."

Clint acknowledged the seriousness of the moment and felt a deep respect for Dr. Jackson's commitment to driving out to this small-town funeral home.

They entered the funeral home, engulfed by a group of people dressed in black. Clint had a good view of the grieving widow as she saw her boss making his way toward her. A smile appeared on her sad face as she realized the CEO of her company had shown up simply to be present with her in this most difficult moment.

Dr. Jackson turned to embrace his employee, and they both began to cry. As the two of them spoke for a few minutes, Clint, feeling a bit out of place, tried to be respectful as he observed the somber moment. Dr. Jackson put his hand on the woman's shoulder, bowed his head, and prayed. The woman nodded along, tears streaming down her face. After the "amen," she took his hand, shook it, and thanked him for coming. She then turned to introduce Dr. Jackson to a family member close by. Clint, by no means a skilled lip reader, couldn't help but see the man mouth the words, "Your CEO?" to the grieving woman with obvious surprise. Dr. Jackson smiled at the man, shook his hand, and turned to walk back to Clint.

"Alright Clint," Dr. Jackson said after he'd made his way back across the room. "I appreciate you allowing me to do that. How about we grab some lunch before our next stop?"

• • •

"Sir, would you like some coffee to go with your dessert?" Clint's thoughts were interrupted by a server holding up a carafe.

Now fully present again at the retirement dinner, Clint smiled and said, "Thank you so much. I would love some coffee. By the way, you're doing a great job this evening. We appreciate you."

All these years later, sitting in this crowded ballroom, Clint could still recall in great detail that trip to the funeral home. Dr. Jackson had never explained exactly who had passed away, and so the Monday following their car ride, Clint asked Sally Thomas, Dr. Jackson's executive assistant, about the woman who had so suddenly lost her husband.

"Oh," said Sally, "she's on our janitorial staff. She's spent more than two decades working nights to keep the hospital clean."

Clint was stunned. They had driven forty-five minutes not to see an executive or a key leader but a member of the hospital cleaning crew.

Sally, who had worked with Dr. Jackson since his arrival at Grace Harbor, grinned and said, "Clint, you will learn that Dr. Jackson works for the good of all the people here. *All* the people."

CHAPTER 4

May I Tell You a Story?

In Clint's opinion, ballroom coffee contended with banquet chicken for the worst possible thing to ingest. After forcing himself to take a few sips, he made eye contact with his wife and checked briefly to see how she was doing. The rest of the table seemed to be caught up in deep conversation. Glancing at the head table, he saw Dr. Jackson sitting there and remembered the first meal they'd shared together—lunch after the funeral home visit.

After the visit, the two men had driven on some side roads before pulling into the parking lot of what appeared to be an abandoned shopping center. By the looks of things, Clint wasn't sure the restaurant was open, let alone prepared to offer a proper lunch.

"I love finding a good hole-in-the-wall restaurant when I'm in these small towns. They know how to make a good meal!" exclaimed Dr. Jackson.

Clint, taking in the dilapidated building, said, "Sounds great—I love trying new things."

His statement bordered on the line between fiction and nonfiction, but he figured he could fake it for a few minutes. He took a deep breath as they entered the restaurant and were seated at a table, hoping the food here was somewhat edible.

After a quick glance at the menu, Dr. Jackson set his menu aside and began to question his young intern once again. "Clint, I appreciate that you have such lofty professional goals for yourself. What draws you to the corporate world? What drives your desire to be a C-suite leader one day?"

Clint, attempting to decide between macaroni and cheese and mashed potatoes and gravy, wasn't prepared for such a question. "Well," he began, "being a leader in a big company means I'll have people who can turn my ideas into profitable products. I guess I'm also looking forward to having a bunch of people who look up to me as their boss." He took a sip of his iced tea, feeling pretty good about his solid answer.

Dr. Jackson responded, "I get it. Many people describe they view leadership that way. It's important for them to have power over people who can get their ideas done so others will see how strong, strategic, and smart they are and hold them in high regard."

"Well, when you say it like that, it doesn't sound quite like it sounded in my head," suggested Clint, who was now feeling a bit nervous.

"Clint," Dr. Jackson said, "I care deeply about teaching people the true core of leadership. I've studied leadership for decades, and I've seen time and time again organizations fail, go under, or get featured in the news for all the wrong reasons. Almost all business collapses can be traced back to poor leadership. Many people mean well, but they mistakenly believe leadership is only about control, power, and position. None of these is inherently bad, but they can be misused."

It appeared Clint had touched a nerve.

Dr. Jackson glanced at his watch and said, "We have a few minutes before our food gets here and a nice drive back to the city in front of us. Do you mind if I tell you a story?"

Sensing this was a rhetorical question, Clint responded, "I love a good story."

"Great. Me too, and this is my favorite story about leadership. In fact, it contains the best definition of leadership in all of history."

A Queen, an Egomaniac, and a Guy Named Mordecai

Over two decades later, Clint could vividly recall the story Dr. Jackson had shared with him over lunch. It had changed the trajectory of Clint's life and shaped his leadership journey.

"Clint," Dr. Jackson had asked, "have you ever heard the story of Esther in the Bible? I mean, I know you've been in church since you were a child, but do you feel like you have a good grasp of this story?"

Clint felt like he should answer in the affirmative, but something told him he needed to be a bit more honest with his new boss. "I know the basics, and I'm pretty sure my football coaches have used the 'For such a time as this' line to try and motivate us to play harder."

Dr. Jackson nodded. "Great. I assumed you were familiar with it. Before I share this story with you, please know I'm going to give you a high-level overview and will undoubtedly gloss over some of the details. I encourage you to read it for yourself sometime. Also, please remember I'm not a theologian, just a longtime student of the Bible and of leadership."

Clint settled into his seat, knowing he wouldn't be going anywhere for a while.

Dr. Jackson began, "The story takes place in Persia, an ancient civilization with vast power. The king of Persia was perhaps the most powerful man on earth in that day. Whatever the king wanted, he got—one way or another. When the king wanted to annex—which is a kind word for *conquer*—a new land, he marched in with his powerful army and took what he wanted. Many people of different nationalities were subject to the king of Persia.

"The story opens with the king, named Xerxes, having a party. It's an all-male party that lasts for days. At one point, a guest suggests the king bring his queen to the party. Do you see the picture? An all-male, likely drunken party, and now one woman is being invited. When the queen receives the summons from her king, she refuses. I have to say, I'm on her side. I wouldn't want to go either. But saying no to a Persian king, even if you *are* his queen, is very serious. It could cost you everything—even your life. And the queen's answer shocked the king.

"At this point in the story, we're given a valuable question about leadership: How does a leader move forward when they don't know what to do? Well, people and organizations are too complicated for any of us to have all the answers. So, when good leaders don't know what to do, they seek advice. Even as far back as the Persian Empire, leaders have used committees and advisory groups. And so the king of Persia, in an act of good leadership, selects a group of men and poses a question to them: What do I do with a queen who says no?"

Dr. Jackson paused as a server arrived with plates full of steaming-hot, delicious-smelling food. Clint's mouth watered as the savory smells filled the air. After Dr. Jackson said a blessing over the meal, Clint dug in and Dr. Jackson continued his story.

"Over the years, I've learned the wonderful benefit of having people advise me in countless areas where I didn't have clear answers. When a group is empowered, a leader should always try to embrace and implement their recommendation. Often, leaders ask a committee for input, only to ignore it. It's easy to see why committees and advisory groups feel abused and undervalued. If you're going to ask a trusted group for advice, take it, *unless* . . ." Dr. Jackson allowed the word to hang in the air.

"Unless . . . what?" asked Clint.

"Unless the leader discovers that the advice is based on a selfish agenda. In this story, that's exactly what happens. The committee recommends the queen be replaced. But note the reason: These bigoted, self-serving men are saying, 'If your queen tells you no and gets away with it, then all of our wives across Persia will begin to tell us no too!' A good leader would have rejected such advice. But Xerxes takes it. And now the search is on for a new queen.

"In Persia, there aren't many criteria for the new queen. But she must look the part—she must be extremely beautiful. The search is massive. Young, beautiful women are recruited. But one woman of rare beauty is discovered. Her beauty is so great that there's no background check performed on her. When Xerxes sees her, he's smitten. Her name is Esther.

"Along with choosing a new queen, the king makes another important selection. He appoints a man who will be second-in-command in all of Persia. This man will be almost like the king in terms of authority and power. The king chose Haman—a name I want you to remember. You'll meet people like him throughout your life. A good leader must be quick to spot the Hamans in his life and organization. They have something I call the leadership disease."

Clint had just taken a big bite of mac and cheese. He nearly laughed at this sudden statement. What in the world was the leadership disease?

Dr. Jackson grinned at Clint's confusion and continued, "The leadership disease is this: Ego out of control, aka excessive pride. The disease is dangerous and abusive. Leaders who have it believe they're right about everything. They strut around wanting everyone to notice them and give them praise. Have you ever seen a leader who fits this description?"

Clint nodded.

"I sure hope you never had to work for someone like this, but you probably will have to deal with one at some point. The only thing worse than working for someone with an ego out of control is living with someone whose ego is out of control. In today's world, the leadership disease is referred to as *narcissism*. Maybe if the story of Esther took place today, Haman would have been diagnosed as a narcissist. He would have felt right at home in today's political climate and social media influencer culture, where out-of-control egos seems to be the norm, not the exception. Everywhere Haman goes, he literally expects people to bow down to him.

"One day, Haman encounters a person who will not bow down. And with his out-of-control ego issues an out-of-control response, Haman decides to kill that man. This brings us to one last major character in the story: Mordecai. I want you to remember that name too, and I hope you aspire to lead from the core the way Mordecai did.

"Haman condemns Mordecai to be killed for refusing to indulge his ego. Remember, Haman is second-in-command, so he can make decisions like this. But this is no ordinary hanging. Haman orders that seventy-five-foot-tall gallows be built. An out-of-control ego always wants to make a show and let everyone see their power.

"During construction of the gallows, Haman discovers Mordecai is not Persian. And so he hatches a new plan. He decides to destroy all of Mordecai's people gathered throughout Persia. Can you imagine? Destroying an entire race of people? Yet, not unheard of. Think about Hitler and the Jewish race. Think of Iraq under the leadership of Saddam Hussein.

"The good news about the leadership disease is that it also destroys the person who has it. It never wins in the long term. It always makes a fatal mistake. Remember that newly appointed queen? She is so beautiful, nobody seems to pay attention to her nationality. Well, she's of the same ethnic background as Mordecai, the same background as the nation whose people are to be destroyed. Haman's zeal has resulted in a death sentence for the new queen. Big mistake! More than that, the person who is to be killed, Mordecai, is the queen's relative.

"Mordecai goes to Esther and urges her to speak to the king on behalf of the Jews. She does, risking her life in the process. In those days, the queen was not allowed to approach the king without being summoned, but she did so anyway. Through Esther's courage and God's favor, the king shows her and her people compassion. And there is an execution, but it's the leader with the out-of-control ego who is put to death, not the humble Mordecai.

"Now, there's a leadership Core principle I want you to remember here. This principle may not be politically correct in how it's expressed, but I think it's important to consider with all of the harshness that's found in this part of the Esther story. Haman's example teaches us this important Core principle: *Keep your ego in check.* Ego out of control is dangerous to everyone around it, and ultimately fatal to the one who has it. To say it in the opposite form: *Leadership is for humble people.* Everyone else ought to stay out of it.

"We see this play out in the story when the king appoints a new leader to replace the deceased Haman. And who gets the job? Mordecai, the man who wouldn't bow down—the one who was almost executed. Mordecai was an exceptional leader. The story says he was respected and loved. He had great credibility. Why? Because he knew and practiced the definition of leadership. Listen to what's said about Mordecai in Esther 10:3 after he became the new second-in-command in all the kingdom: '[He] was held in high esteem by his many fellow Jews, because *he worked for the good of his people* and spoke up for the welfare of all the Jews.'

"That's the best summary I've ever heard or read about leadership. Leaders work *for the good of the people* they lead. That's all there is to it. Leading is not about the welfare of the leader; it's about the welfare of those being led! This principle translates to every aspect of life. Parents are leaders who work for the good of their children. Husbands are leaders who work for the good of their wives. Wives are leaders who work for the good of their husbands. Presidents, CEOs, ministers, department heads, supervisors, they all have one job—to work for the good of the people. Clint," Dr. Jackson addressed the young man directly, "if I asked you who you work for, what would you say?"

"Well," said Clint, setting down his fork beside the empty plate, "you, sir."

"Of course," smiled Dr. Jackson. "That's true. It's natural to name the person above us on the organizational chart, whether it's a manager, the board of directors, or the president. But leaders don't look up the chart—they look *down* the chart! A leader's job is to work for the good of the people, and the better you serve those who follow you, the better the organization, the better the profits, the better the morale. *Everything* is better.

"These two principles, Clint, are the starting place for the leadership Core: Leaders work for the good of the people, and they recognize that an ego out of control leads to destruction. I think you're now ready to move to the next principle in building your Core."

"There's more?" Clint exclaimed.

Dr. Jackson smiled and said, "Yes, and I don't know about you, but I could use a pick-me-up right about now. Do you want to get some ice cream before we head back to the city?"

If I Perish, I Perish

I hear there's a chance they won't survive another year."

Now enjoying dessert, the folks seated at Clint's table were discussing a local business that, rumor had it, was struggling.

Clint asked, "Why do you think they're struggling so much? They've been in business for a long time."

Jerry Martin, another local business leader, summarized what he had been hearing around town: "They've had trouble keeping up with the times and the competition. They have a solid team, but no one can convince the founder to go in a new direction."

"It sounds like the only new direction they're going is downward," chimed in Mrs. Martin, eliciting a nervous chuckle from the group.

Clint said, "Look, they've been a successful business for decades. All of us have probably purchased something from them at one time or another, right?"

Everyone nodded.

"And sure, factors like costs and supply chain changes impact profit," he continued. "Plus, that new store on the other side of town has probably siphoned off some of their business. But since their products are good, and they have a consistent local customer base, my guess is it's a leadership issue. Most organizations rise and fall on leadership. I'm not saying the leaders they have are bad people; they may just have developed some significant blind spots over the years.

"First, it seems they've failed to embrace the reality that's right in front of them. Second, if I were a betting man, and don't worry, Kristen, I'm not," he said, winking at his wife, "I would bet a lot of money the founder struggles to lead with his ears. They also may be suffering from a lack of courage."

Clint had the table's full attention.

Jerry asked, "What in the world does it mean to lead with your ears?"

Clint, recognizing he was beginning a lecture no one had asked for, paused and said, "Can I tell you a story to explain what I mean?"

Most of the table—except for Kristen, who had a hunch she'd heard this story before—nodded.

Clint began, "Do you all remember the story of Esther in the Bible?" More nods. Clint went on, "Esther, a teenage beauty queen who found herself the queen of Persia, was married to a king who chose a leader with an ego that was out of control. Haman, the second-in-command, issued a decree that all the Jews throughout the empire should be slaughtered. Mordecai, Esther's cousin, sent word through one of Esther's servants to alert her of the edict, begging her to act on behalf of her people."

Mrs. Martin interrupted, "Oh, I love this part—where he says, 'Who knows that you have been put in this position for such a time as this.' Right, Clint? I have that quote on a sign in the entryway of my house."

"Yes, that's correct," Clint affirmed. "Mordecai put the truth in front of Esther as clearly as he could. After Mordecai's message, Esther had a decision to make. She could ignore the facts in front of her, or she could embrace the truth, lead with her ears, and summon an uncommon amount of courage to act. I doubt Esther had ever been through leadership development programs or strategic planning sessions." The table chuckled at Clint's joke. "But she was wise enough to know she couldn't ignore the truth. She knew she had to act.

"One of the most underappreciated parts of this story is what happened next. She sent word to Mordecai, encouraging him to join her and her servants in fasting for three days as she prepared herself mentally for the task ahead. She then spoke a line that gives me chills: 'When this is done, I will go to the king, even though it is against the law. And if I perish, I perish.'" Now in full speech mode, Clint repeated the last line for dramatic effect: *"And if I perish, I perish."*

Looking at Jerry, Clint said, "This teenage beauty queen led with her ears. She listened to the cries of her people, embraced the truth, and then possessed the courage to do whatever it took. If that isn't core to leadership, I don't know what is. If all leaders could approach challenges like Esther did, there would be a lot fewer discussions around ballroom dinner tables about the latest organizations that have surprisingly failed."

The faces around the table now appeared contemplative. It was clear that Clint's impromptu leadership speech had struck a nerve.

As the servers came to clear the empty dessert plates, Kristen excused herself to go to the restroom. As she stood, she put her hand on Clint's shoulder, leaned in, and whispered in his ear, "I'll be right back. Please save your next lecture for when I return."

The Coach and the Fog

Clint was impressed by the turnout in the ballroom, both the quantity and quality of the guest list. He had always been impressed by the diversity of people who claimed Dr. Jackson as a friend and mentor. Now it seemed the entire city had shown up to honor this man who had always shown honor to others.

Clint smiled, recalling the first road trip they'd ever taken together. Dr. Jackson had been so kind, helping Clint with his wheelchair as they left the restaurant and returned to the car. "We might hit a little traffic on our way to the next destination," Dr. Jackson had said, turning onto the highway. "This should give me enough time to address a few more Core Leadership principles before we arrive at the university for the speech."

Clint, still unclear on what Dr. Jackson's speaking engagement was all about, buckled up literally and figuratively. *He must be practicing his talk on me*, Clint thought, deciding to play along.

But before Dr. Jackson continued his speech, his cell phone rang. "Right on time," he said. "Clint, I hope you don't mind, but I need to take this short call. You'll be able to hear it over the speaker phone, but I want you to listen in."

He then answered the phone: "Good afternoon, Michael, how are you doing today?"

"Bill, I'm doing well, thanks for asking," the man on the other end responded. "Is this still a good time for our weekly check-in?"

Dr. Jackson said, "Sure. I'm driving between appointments, and I have my new intern in the car with me. He won't mind if we chat for a few minutes."

Clint, curious about who Michael was and why a man like Dr. Jackson needed a weekly check-in, leaned forward in his seat to listen.

"Bill," Michael said, "how are you finding your way through the fog this week physically? I know you've had some extra travel since our last call. Did you take care of yourself on the road?"

Dr. Jackson replied, "Well, I did okay. I worked out a couple of times at the hotel while I was away and tried to eat well."

Michael laughed and said, "Not too much ice cream, I hope!"

Dr. Jackson winked at Clint and said, "Not too much. I did succumb to a little peer pressure this afternoon from my young intern friend here, but I did pretty well over the last week."

Clint felt like an accomplice to some kind of ice-cream crime.

Michael then asked, "Well, how about emotionally? Did you find some ways to recharge your emotional battery?"

Clint was surprised by Michael's invasive questions, but Dr. Jackson didn't skip a beat. He told Michael he and his wife, June, had spent some quality time together over the weekend, including date night with close friends on Saturday and church small group on Sunday.

Michael asked a third question of Dr. Jackson: "Bill, what about the spiritual tank? How are you keeping that reservoir filled this week?"

Clint, now immersed in the conversation, was eager to hear Dr. Jackson's answer.

"Michael, I've reread some familiar Bible stories this week, looking for leadership lessons. I've also spent some extra time praying for wisdom and discernment about some big decisions coming up at Grace Harbor."

"That's great, Bill," responded Michael. "I'm proud of you for putting what we had discussed into practice. Keep cutting through the fog this week. At our next check-in, I want to discuss plans for our half-day group session next month."

"Thank you, Michael. I'll carry on," said Dr. Jackson.

"You and your intern have a safe drive. And don't stop for any more ice cream," were Michael's last words of wisdom before ending the call.

"Okay," Clint jumped in as soon as Dr. Jackson hung up, "can I ask a few questions?"

Dr. Jackson nodded.

"First of all, who is Michael? And why is he meddling in your personal life?"

Dr. Jackson chuckled and said, "Michael is my executive leadership coach. I've known him for fifteen years. He's spent countless hours helping me become the best leader I can possibly be. He's helped me realize some things about myself that were holding me back—and consequently were holding back our team at Grace Harbor."

Clint, wide-eyed, asked, "A coach? I thought *you* were the leadership expert."

With a serious look on his face, Dr. Jackson responded, "A leader must be coachable. No one person has all the answers—even those at the very top. It took me a while to understand that. Leaders must be lifelong learners. And we always need people in our lives who can give us perspective."

"I think I get that," said Clint, "but why did he ask you such personal questions? What do ice cream and fog have to do with leading Grace Harbor?"

Clint's comment made Dr. Jackson laugh out loud. "Clint, often leaders find themselves very tired, some may even say fatigued, due to the stress and strain of leadership. The fatigue causes a sort of 'fog' to set in. Their vision gets hazy, making it difficult for them to move forward, make decisions, or navigate stressful situations. When people are stuck in the fog for a long time, they begin to flirt, if you will, with poor decisions. They start cutting corners or treating people poorly."

Clint nodded, eyebrows furrowed as he processed this information.

"Early in my career, I had trouble with the fog," Dr. Jackson continued. "It dragged me down at work and impacted me as a husband and a father. I felt burnt out and wasn't sure what to do. Then I met Michael through a friend. At first, I was hesitant to be coached, but after our first few sessions, I realized I needed to humble myself and accept some help before I got lost in the fog for good. Michael has taught me many 'fog-cutting' strategies over the years."

"But what does that actually look like in real life?" Clint asked.

"Picture three tanks," Dr. Jackson explained. "One for your physical well-being, one for your emotional well-being, and one for your spiritual well-being. By keeping each tank full, leaders have plenty of energy and clarity to keep the fatigue, fog, and flirtation at bay."

Clint nodded, looking out the window. "It reminds me of something my football coach always used to say."

"Oh?" said Dr. Jackson. "What's that?"

"Pace yourself and extend the game. As a player, you need to manage your energy so you can keep playing the game, especially when things are neck and neck. Fatigue can be the difference between a caught pass or a dropped ball, which can result in a win or a loss."

"I like that very much, Clint," said Dr. Jackson, smiling. "Pace yourself and extend the game."

The two men were silent for a moment before Clint said, "The third tank, the spiritual one, is confusing to me. Aren't leaders supposed to leave spiritual matters at the door when they get to work, for the sake of those who may not believe the same way they do?"

This question grabbed Dr. Jackson's attention. "Clint," he began, "I appreciate that question. It's one that many people struggle with. When the third tank is depleted, it sets a leader up for pride. And pride leads to an out-of-control ego, which leads to destruction. Being in God's Word, praying, and spending time with other believers keeps me humble and able to better serve those I lead."

Clint, attempting to connect the dots of the day's lessons, asked, "Does this fit into the Esther story somehow too?"

Dr. Jackson grinned and said, "I'm glad you asked. It isn't as obvious as some of the other Core principles we've discussed, but it's in there. Do you remember the part of the story where Mordecai learned of Haman's plans to destroy the Jewish people? The Bible tells us when the news got out, there was great mourning among the Jews, with fasting, weeping, and wailing.

"You could say that at this point, the 'fog' of the situation was thick around all the Jews, especially Esther and Mordecai, as they weighed their options. But even though Esther didn't have a 'Michael' in her life, she found a way to cut through the stress and gain some perspective. She asked her servants and Mordecai to join her in the spiritual act of fasting for three days. Fasting was a strategy Esther used to fill her spiritual tank and cut through the fog, preparing her for a tough situation that required clearheaded courage."

"I guess you could say that Esther was coachable too," Clint observed. "She was willing to listen to Mordecai's advice instead of just relying on her own perspective."

"You're right," Dr. Jackson agreed. "And not only are you right, but I also think you're catching on to the leadership Core principles in this rich story. In one example, we've seen two lessons: Be coachable, pace yourself, and extend the game. I suggest you commit these principles to memory as you grow as a leader."

Clint nodded, a thoughtful look on his face.

"Now, let's get inside and get ready for this speech," said Dr. Jackson, putting the car in park.

Clint, surprised they had already reached the university, unbuckled his seat belt, excited to hear Dr. Jackson's talk.

• • •

Present-day Clint was interrupted from his reverie by Kristen, who had returned from the restroom, putting her hand on his shoulder. "Looks like the program's about to start. I'm sure Dr. Jackson is going to give a great speech."

"Yes," Clint agreed, "I'm certain he will."

As Good as Our People

As the master of ceremonies walked up to the podium, a respectful silence filled the room. Clint leaned back in his chair, looking forward to the special evening celebrating his mentor.

The emcee directed the crowd's attention to the screen, where a video tribute of Dr. Jackson's career at Grace Harbor began to play. Clint knew his mentor was uncomfortable with all the attention. He loved to celebrate others but had a hard time accepting celebration on his own behalf.

As the video clips rolled across the screen, Clint grew emotional. His mind drifted back to that very first car ride with his mentor. Even then, Dr. Jackson had modeled what it looked like to cheer others on.

• • •

Dr. Jackson pushed Clint's wheelchair across campus, hurrying to reach their destination. Clint felt bad for adding to the time crunch.

"I'm sorry you have to push me," he said. "I hate that I'm making you late for your speech."

"*My* speech?" questioned Dr. Jackson. "Oh, I'm not giving a speech today. We're racing to *hear* a speech." Before Clint could voice his confusion, Dr. Jackson said, "Here's the room we're looking for."

They arrived just as the event was beginning. Sliding into seats in the back row of an auditorium-style classroom, Dr. Jackson and Clint joined a group of about twenty other people. Clint was surprised to see such a small crowd gathered for an event that was worth a CEO's time. A professor at the university stood to welcome the audience and began her remarks: "Todd has worked so hard in this master's program. We're thrilled to hear about his capstone project."

It dawned on Clint that he and Dr. Jackson had come all this way to hear from . . . a graduate student? He looked at the screen and read the title slide: "The Role of Healthcare Informatics in Improving Patient Outcomes in Faith-Based Regional Hospital Systems: A Quantitative Study." Knowing nothing about the speaker or the topic, Clint did his best to appear interested.

The host brought Todd to the front of the auditorium, and those in attendance gave a polite round of applause. Todd, looking nervous, scanned the room and made eye contact with Dr. Jackson in the back row. A wide smile filled the grad student's face. With confidence, he walked up to the podium and begin his presentation.

For forty-five minutes, Todd shared an incredible amount of data and research. Clint got lost in the details and found himself wondering who this guy was and why they were there. When Todd clicked through the last slide and ended his presentation, the audience gave him another round of applause. The professor who had welcomed everyone to the event returned to the podium and said a few more words, expressing pride in her student and his work, before inviting the attendees to a reception in the foyer.

Dr. Jackson then wheeled Clint to the reception, positioning him by the dessert table. He leaned over and said, "I need to catch Todd for a few minutes before we head back to the car." Clint watched as his mentor made his way over to the grad student. Dr. Jackson shook hands and chatted with a few people as he waited patiently for his turn to speak with Todd, who had now been joined by what appeared to be his wife and two young children.

When Dr. Jackson reached the front of the line, Todd beamed and gave him a big hug. He turned and introduced the hospital CEO to his wife and kids. Dr. Jackson then put his hands on Todd's shoulders and looked him in the eye as he spoke. Todd looked misty-eyed as he nodded his head, taking in the CEO's words of congratulations. Patting Todd on the back one more time, Dr. Jackson then made his way back to Clint. "You didn't sneak too many cookies over here while I was visiting, did you?" he asked playfully.

"No sir, I didn't want to be a bad influence on you again," Clint said.

Back in the car, Dr. Jackson said, "Wasn't that great? I'm so proud of Todd. Having a master's degree is going to open up a lot of great opportunities for him when he leaves Grace Harbor."

"So," Clint began, "Todd works for Grace Harbor? And he's leaving? I'm confused. I thought he might be a relative of yours. Why did we come all this way to see his presentation?"

"I assumed you'd have some questions." Dr. Jackson laughed. "Todd Perkins has been a part of Grace Harbor since graduating from college eight years ago. He's extremely intelligent. He has a deep appreciation for healthcare and came to the hospital to work on the administrative side of things. His team leader quickly realized that while Todd was an excellent employee and could have a great career in our hospital system, his analytical mind was better suited for a career in research, which Grace Harbor isn't designed to do. After about six years, Todd had pretty much maxed out his opportunities on our team. He was stuck in the fog. He'd hit the ceiling and was teetering on burnout because he wasn't being challenged or fulfilled by his work.

"I was grateful when his supervisor brought Todd's situation to our senior leadership team's attention. We've all seen talented young people leave our organization because it was the only option they thought they had. I've sat in the conference room listening to my colleagues bellyache and moan about the challenges of retaining emerging talent. I'm usually composed in these situations, but this time, I needed to get their attention. So, I pounded my fist on the table. They looked at me like deer caught in the headlights! Once I got their attention, I reminded them that we're only as good as our people and we needed to better understand how to motivate and maximize the giftings of each employee so they could better live out their own stories. Our goal should be to see people thrive, using their God-given talents.

"The leadership team took my words to heart. They came to our next meeting with a set of strategies designed to help our people flourish—not so they can be what we need them to be but so they can be who God designed them to be. Todd was our first case study. We offered to give him more flexible work so he could pursue a master's degree. We saw so much potential in him and wanted him to eventually land at a research institute focused on helping hospitals like ours."

Clint interrupted, "So you basically helped him improve his personal situation, knowing he'd leave Grace Harbor? I've never seen that strategy in any of my management textbooks."

"I know, Clint. It's a bit unorthodox, for sure. But at Grace Harbor, we have a big vision. We don't just want to help our organization. We want to benefit a wide range of small regional hospitals over the next thirty-plus years."

Clint, still a bit puzzled, said, "I get it, but don't you still need to consider the return on your investment? How will it do you any good if you train people only to send them elsewhere?"

Dr. Jackson said, "I know it's counterintuitive, but the results speak for themselves. In the two years he was part of this program, Todd has been as productive as any employee in his department, even with his flexible schedule. He became engaged in his work and no longer felt burned out. He took what he was learning in school and applied those ideas to Grace Harbor, saving us a lot of money and improving our patient experience in the process. By investing in his growth, we also invested in Grace Harbor. Our leadership team is sad to see him go, but we know Todd's future research will benefit us in ways we can't even imagine now. I would much rather he leave equipped to make a difference in the world than walk away burned out and bitter that we didn't care about him as a human being."

Clint nodded; the puzzle pieces were starting to fall into place.

"Clint," Dr. Jackson said, "do you remember that quote about Mordecai from our discussion of Esther a few hours ago?"

Clint stammered, "Something like, 'He was good to the people?'"

"Close," Dr. Jackson said. "But Mordecai was more than just 'good' or 'nice' to his people. Scripture says in the last verse of the book of Esther that Mordecai was held in high esteem by many of his fellow Jews, because he worked for the good of his people and spoke up for the welfare of all the Jews. He worked for their good, Clint. Not just so they could contribute to his agenda or the strategic plan. We came to Todd's presentation because my job as CEO of Grace Harbor is to work for the good of the people, speaking up for their welfare and supporting them when they give speeches—even when they use words I don't fully understand."

Clint glanced at Dr. Jackson and saw him grinning, as usual, as he navigated traffic.

Two Great Days

That famous Bill Jackson grin continued to show up in the still shots and video clips that flashed across the screens as the tribute played. Clint recognized many of the images. He had attended most of the events that were being highlighted. He was even in a few of the pictures, smiling alongside Dr. Jackson.

Clint no longer wondered why Dr. Jackson was always so joyful. He had learned that lesson many years ago, sitting in the Grace Harbor parking lot after their memorable day trip.

• • •

Dr. Jackson pulled into his customary spot in the back of the lot. Clint, gearing up for the long trek, unbuckled his seat belt and reached for the door handle.

"Clint," said Dr. Jackson, "wait just a moment. We had a long day, and we talked about a lot of important things. Do you have any questions about what we discussed?"

Clint was hit by a wave of fatigue. He hadn't been this active since before his accident. As he replayed the day's events, he could only come up with one question. He hesitated to ask it, nervous about how it would come across to this powerful CEO. Finally, he said, "Why do you do all of this? I mean, why do you do what you do?"

Dr. Jackson relaxed in the driver's seat. He took a deep breath and said, "Clint, that's the most important question you could ask me. It's also the most important question for you to ask yourself on a regular basis."

Clint didn't think the question was profound—he was genuinely curious. Dr. Jackson did not behave as Clint imagined a CEO would. Granted, Clint hadn't had too many interactions with CEOs in the past. He'd certainly never eaten ice cream with one before.

"I will answer your question, but first, I want to tell you something that a mentor of mine shared with me a long time ago," said Dr. Jackson. "Early in my career as a surgeon, I was at a professional impasse. I had spent years in school, training, studying, and working toward this one goal. I had wanted to become a surgeon since I was a young boy. After school and training, I did a surgical residency at a very prestigious hospital in the Northeast. But I wasn't happy there. I enjoyed working with patients, but something was missing. After trying to make it work for two years, I found myself completely miserable."

"Caught in the fog?" asked Clint.

"Well, maybe at first," Dr. Jackson nodded. "But it was deeper than that. I was struggling with my sense of purpose. Thankfully, I was 'voluntold' by the chief medical officer to serve on a committee dedicated to working on hospital-wide initiatives. That first committee meeting changed the course of my life. In the conference room were a mix of doctors and administrators. Most of the doctors weren't thrilled about being there, but I was exhilarated. I loved hearing about the different initiatives and considering ways we could make our systems more efficient.

"That night, I told my wife, June, all about it, describing in detail the topics discussed and the potential changes that could improve the hospital. As a surgeon, I felt like I could offer a unique perspective to better serve our patients and employees. I still remember my sweet wife looking at me over the dinner table, smiling as she said, 'This is the first time I've seen you excited about work since you graduated from medical school!'

"That night as I lay in bed, I could still feel myself grinning. I felt like I had accomplished something meaningful, and I hadn't felt like that in a long time. A few months passed, and I consistently found myself looking forward to those committee meetings—way more than a normal person should look forward to them!

"One weekend, I was at a men's Bible study, catching up with a retired friend. He had been a very successful lawyer early in his career before taking a role as the leader of a nonprofit organization that provided legal aid to single mothers. I asked him a question like the one you asked me a few minutes ago: Why did he do what he did, giving up a successful career to be in the nonprofit space?

"With a serious look on his face, he said, 'Bill, there are two great days in your life—the day you are born and the day you realize why you were born.' He went on to explain that the first great day—the one where we are born—should never be taken for granted. On that day, we were blessed with God-given talents, gifts, strengths, and abilities to make a difference in the world. But the second great day—the day we realize *why* we were born—is one many people don't get. It's not about working a specific job or career—it's about fulfilling a divine purpose that transcends our professional pursuits. Whether you're a lawyer, a surgeon, a finance expert, a teacher, or a stay-at-home parent, God has called each of us to something bigger. When we embrace that role, we can be a part of changing the world.

"The committee was instrumental in helping me learn my purpose. I was drawn away from surgery and into administration. June and I talked and prayed, and we decided to look for an opportunity to live out my purpose differently. Providentially, a door opened at a small faith-based hospital in Arkansas. They were hiring a medical director, and I got the job. I fell in love with the work and the people, and I felt a great sense of calling in my new vocation from the moment I arrived. That move led me to become the CEO of that hospital, which opened the door for me to come work for the people of Grace Harbor."

Dr. Jackson paused, a look of gratitude on his face. "Leadership," he continued, "is full of ups and downs. But I still smile when I think of how blessed I am to lead an organization like Grace Harbor. Walking in your purpose brings a joy deeper than circumstances. To lead from the core, you must understand and stay connected to your sense of purpose and how it ties into your organization's unique mission.

"Clint," he said with authority, "*that* is why I do what I do."

Clint, surprised by how emotional he felt, said, "It's like the part in Esther that suggests she had been put in that situation for such a time as this."

Dr. Jackson looked Clint straight in the eye and said, "It's also why I walked into your hospital room after your accident to convince you to do an internship with me here at Grace Harbor."

Clint hadn't seen that one coming. But Dr. Jackson was done answering questions for the day. He got out of the car, unloaded Clint's wheelchair, and offered to push him back to the hospital.

Truth and Grace

The crowd applauded as the video montage concluded, bringing Clint back to the moment. He joined in the clapping, trying to make it look like he'd been paying attention.

The master of ceremonies introduced the next speaker, the chair of the Grace Harbor Board, Tom Kinsey. Tom had been associated with Grace Harbor for at least three decades as the leader of a large supplier for the hospital. He was a generous donor, a board member, and—most recently—the spouse of a patient. His wife, Betty, had been in and out of the hospital fighting serious illnesses for several months before passing away last year. As a beloved member of the community, Betty's suffering was mourned by all, but none of her friends were as heartbroken as Dr. Bill and June Jackson. They had grown extremely close over the years. Dr. Jackson had recruited Tom to join the board, and the two couples hoped to spend their retirement years deepening their friendship.

Clint had known Tom for a long time. In fact, he specifically remembered the day he met Tom, because it was the same day he was medically released by his doctors to walk without crutches. All summer, he would start his day in physical therapy, rebuilding his core strength before reporting for intern duties. Today, he felt like a free man. He could not wait to get to the office and show off his slow but steady walk to the friends he had made at the office.

That summer had been a true blessing for Clint. At Grace Harbor, he'd learned what it took to run a faith-based hospital. He spent meaningful time with Dr. Bill Jackson, gaining insight about how to lead from the Core. Though eager to return to campus and cheer on his former teammates, he felt a surprising sadness as the internship neared its end. The friendships and lessons he'd gained made leaving harder than he'd expected. Grace Harbor had left its mark.

As Clint entered the suite, he was shocked to see his team standing in the reception area with streamers and balloons. They cheered wildly as he walked in, no crutches in sight, slowly making his way through a cloud of confetti. He saw Dr. Jackson standing in the middle of the small group, fists full of confetti.

Clint was deeply honored but not surprised. He knew Dr. Jackson well enough by now to expect him at a celebration like this. Nobody, not even a summer intern, was too insignificant for his attention. Clint had seen this group celebrate everything from marriage engagements to the baptisms of employees' children. They'd even hosted a celebration for an employee who had paid off her mortgage early by working extra hours. Clint knew the corporate world awaiting him after college might look very different, but he was determined to find a role in an organization that prioritized its people like Grace Harbor did.

As he walked around the room showing off his new stride, Clint thanked everyone for their help throughout the summer. He looked at Dr. Jackson and said, "Guess you won't have to push me across the parking lot anymore."

"Oh brother," joked Dr. Jackson. "I guess I'll have to start going to the gym again."

Clint hugged the CEO. At the beginning of the summer, Clint had barely known what a mentor was. Now he believed he had the best one in the world.

"Clint," said Dr. Jackson, "I know you can't wait to walk all over the place today, but what do you say you and I take a ride? I have a few things I need to take care of."

Clint said, "I'll get all the steps I need today, just getting to your car."

Minutes later, as they were exiting the hospital, Dr. Jackson made what had become a trademark comment in Clint's direction: "Clint, I've been thinking."

Of course you have, Clint thought to himself.

Dr. Jackson went on to say, "I do hope you've enjoyed your time at Grace Harbor this summer and learned a thing or two about life in the hospital world. But more importantly, I hope you've learned a lot about yourself and what it takes to lead from the Core. We've all enjoyed having you around. Your curiosity and willingness to learn will serve you well in the future."

"Well, to tell you the truth," Clint said, "when you first offered me the position, I wasn't sure I would like it. I especially wasn't sure about the car-ride, hole-in-the-wall, ancient-Bible-story, Core-principle approach to leadership training. But now, looking back, I consider this one of the best experiences of my life. I'm so grateful for the lessons you've taught me, and even more so for the examples you've shown me this summer."

Dr. Jackson's grin grew extra wide. He steered the car into the parking lot of an office building that Clint didn't recognize. "Clint," he said, "I appreciate your kind words, and I do hope that you have learned more from my actions than my words. If not, I have failed you as a leader and a mentor. I also should say that we are not done with the lessons. Today may be a tough one, but it's essential to the leadership Core."

Dr. Jackson parked the car, unbuckled his seat belt, did a quick check of his tie in the rearview mirror, and then turned to Clint. "Do you remember earlier this summer when we talked about how leaders must embrace the truth and act with courage?"

Clint, who had been going over the Core principles in his head for the past ten weeks every night before he went to bed, nodded.

Dr. Jackson continued, "Do you recall that moment in the Esther story where she decides to embrace the truth? After she fasts and prepares to appeal to the king, there's an easy-to-skip-over part of the story that applies to our study of the leadership Core. Two different times, she finds herself in the presence of King Xerxes, risking her life. Now remember, at this point, she knows Haman is planning a genocide of her people. Yet instead of just going to the king, kicking and screaming, she approaches him with a sense of poise and, dare I say, grace. She uses language like 'If it pleases the king' and 'If I have found favor with you, your Majesty' to win him over. Esther knows she must share truth with grace mixed with a proper length of time."

Clint got excited. "The numbers guy in me hears that like a formula! Truth plus Grace over Time."

"I like it! And today, Clint, we get to put that formula to the test. We'll pair it with another Core principle: Show up with grace. How we handle ourselves matters. It makes an impression on those we lead and can be the determining factor between success and failure. You'll spend the rest of your career developing your leadership presence. Leadership is messy. We're regularly forced to handle challenging situations where there's a lot at stake. We don't always choose our circumstances, but we can always choose how we respond to those circumstances. Now, I want you to come with me." Dr. Jackson reached for the door handle. "And don't worry—I don't expect this to take long."

"Dr. Jackson," Clint asked humbly, "do you mind telling me what we're here to do so I'm not surprised by the situation?"

"That's fair," Dr. Jackson responded. "I'm here to cut ties with one of our longest-serving vendors. We'll be meeting with one of my favorite people in the city, the company's CEO, and one of our donors, so I can share the news with him directly."

Clint's eyes widened. He felt a knot forming in his gut.

After entering the waiting room, Clint recognized where he was: the headquarters for the Bright Light Supply Company, which provided paper products and medical supplies that Grace Harbor used. Clint didn't know the exact numbers, but he did know the volume of business they did with Bright Light was enormous.

An executive assistant invited Dr. Jackson and Clint to follow her to the CEO's conference room. When she asked if they would like anything to drink, Dr. Jackson quickly said, "No thanks, we may not be here long."

Clint glanced around, noticing a shelf full of awards Bright Light had received for outstanding business and community involvement.

He even noticed a small plaque on the wall from Grace Harbor, acknowledging their years of valued partnership.

Clint hadn't been this nervous since he had asked a beautiful young lady named Kristen to attend a football awards banquet with him last winter. As his nerves rose, he looked over at Dr. Jackson, whose eyes were shut and head was bowed.

Was he praying? This was going to be worse than Clint thought!

Soon, a man who appeared to be close to Dr. Jackson's age walked in and greeted them, shaking their hands and asking them again if they needed something to drink. Clint had never wanted water more dearly in all his life, not even during two-a-day football practices. But he knew he had to decline.

"Bill," the CEO started, "I was told you needed to meet as soon as possible to discuss a situation. I hope everything is okay at the hospital."

Dr. Jackson replied with his standard grin in place. "I'm so glad you were able to squeeze me in—I know you're a busy guy. I hope you know how much we value your company and the long-term relationship we've enjoyed between our organizations. I also hope you know I consider you to be a great leader, and I count you as a friend."

"Bill," the man said, "my feelings are mutual for both Grace Harbor and you, but I'm a bit concerned there may be a reason as to why you're here today."

"You're right," Dr. Jackson calmly answered. "Earlier this week, our accounting team discovered a significant set of overcharges your company has been invoicing. This has been going on for more than six months. While the individual invoices are not large enough to draw a lot of attention, due to the large volume of business between our organizations, the total amounts have added up to hundreds of thousands of dollars."

"Now, Bill," the man responded sternly, "are you accusing my people of stealing? Come on—you know we wouldn't do that on purpose. There's got to be an explanation."

"Of course," Dr. Jackson began, "I don't believe you would do this intentionally, but I have reason to think someone on your team may be tampering with the numbers for personal gain. About five months ago, a discrepancy was flagged and logged by one of our accountants. She recently raised it with someone she trusts on your team—someone who confirmed the transactions aren't in your system and didn't recognize the person who first took the call. I'm sorry to share this with you, but until you get things sorted out, we're going to move our business to one of your competitors."

"Hold on, Bill!" the now-angry CEO raised his voice. "You can't just come in here and accuse us of some scam! We have contracts and a reputation to uphold."

"I'm not accusing you—I'm stating the facts. Since you're just now hearing about this, and it's been reported multiple times over the past few months, I'm concerned there may be something else at play. I must take what I know and make the best decision I can for our organization."

The CEO's eyes narrowed as he stared at Dr. Jackson.

"We're going to take a break from our working relationship so we can assess the situation," said Dr. Jackson. "I hope that over time, as trust is rebuilt, we can do business together again."

Clint sat stunned as he watched the two CEOs go back and forth. One of them, the apparent victim, was speaking calmly, truthfully, and with a sense of hope for reconciliation. The other, the man whose company had taken advantage of another, or at best had some bad invoicing practices, was responding with anger, defensiveness, and pride.

Dr. Jackson stood up and reached out his hand to the other man. The CEO jumped out of his seat and said, "You can save your handshake for the courtroom! You've broken the contract."

Clint, realizing he was now the only one sitting, rose and stood behind Dr. Jackson, who paused before walking toward the door. Dr. Jackson looked back at his longtime friend and said, "I know this is hard. It is for me too. I would love to grab breakfast with you in a few weeks to discuss this further."

As they exited the office, Clint looked back at the nameplate on the door: *Tom Kinsey, Chief Executive Officer*.

The intern and his mentor walked through the waiting room and the parking lot and got in the car. They drove in silence for a few minutes. Words weren't necessary. Finally, as they neared their next stop, Dr. Jackson looked over at his young mentee and said, "I told you leadership was messy."

Clint, his heart racing, couldn't have agreed more.

"How about we grab some lunch?" Dr. Jackson suggested. "I know a great little hole-in-the-wall in this neighborhood."

A Future Here

The fact that Tom Kinsey stood on stage at Dr. Jackson's retirement party was evidence of the power of reconciliation. Tom's remarks were full of gratitude for the many lessons about life and leadership he had learned from his friend.

"Some of those lessons," Tom said, pausing as he became emotional, "were harder to learn than others. But with Bill, you're always going to get someone who is not just willing but courageous enough to share the truth. Yet he does so with grace. I'm grateful to have done business with him for most of the past three decades. More than that, I'm so glad he is my friend."

Clint, sitting in the audience, thought back to the first time he'd met Tom Kinsey. The story hadn't ended the day he and Dr. Jackson left an angry Tom in his office.

On the last day of Clint's internship, he walked around the hospital saying his goodbyes. He thanked as many people as he could for his experience that summer, both as an intern and a patient. When Clint returned to the administrative offices, he saw Dr. Jackson at Sally's desk, picking up a few forms and pieces of mail. Dr. Jackson smiled when he saw his intern. "Well, I suspect I need to give you an update on something. Why don't you come back to my office for a few minutes?"

Clint eagerly walked past Sally's desk and joined the Grace Harbor CEO in his office. He sat in a chair next to the small circular table and watched as Dr. Jackson put his suit coat on a hanger. He seemed even more cheerful than normal this morning.

"Clint," Dr. Jackson said, "it's hard to believe this is your last day with us! I want to discuss something with you before you go—but first, I wanted to let you know that Tom Kinsey and I had breakfast early this morning."

"Well, I don't see any bruises, black eyes, or blood on you. I assume either Mr. Kinsey was in a better mood than when we left his office, or you decided to meet in a public spot for breakfast," Clint joked.

Dr. Jackson, not nearly as amused as Clint had hoped he would be, took it in stride and said, "Clint, Tom let me know that after our conversation, he went directly to his team to find out what was going on. They uncovered a sophisticated financial scam. The person involved admitted to it and said Grace Harbor was the first target, but he planned to keep scamming other large clients. The police are now involved. Things will be chaotic for Bright Light for a while."

"Wow, that's terrible," offered Clint. "I'm glad you were able to bring the issue to light, even if it was difficult."

"Tom said something very similar to that," replied Dr. Jackson. "But more than that, he wanted to apologize for the way he responded when I confronted him. He owned the fact that his concern for his reputation should not have trumped his concern for us as a client."

"Wow!" Clint responded. "That Truth plus Grace over Time stuff is something, isn't it?"

"It's a core element of leadership, Clint, no more important than the other principles we've discussed. But it does serve as a connecting point for many of them. It involves having control over one's ego, leading with your ears, being coachable, putting people first, and having a sense of purpose and vision for the bigger picture in life."

"Does this mean we can go back to doing business with them?" asked Clint.

"In time, we may do so. But I need to see where things stand with a contract we signed with another supplier. Now, let's talk a little about you, Clint." Dr. Jackson sat up in his chair. "What have you learned this summer about yourself? What have you learned about leadership?"

Clint, now used to Dr. Jackson's impromptu questions, said, "Sir, I am so grateful for this place. The people of Grace Harbor have a real sense of unity and know their purpose. I can also tell they feel appreciated by you and the other leaders. It's almost as if the culture here is—dare I say this about a hospital—a healthy one."

Dr. Jackson laughed and said, "Well, that's good to hear. If we're healthy as an organization, it allows us to better serve our patients and, well—dare I say—it helps them to be healthier too."

Clint said, "I see what you did there."

"Thanks," said a now-smiling Dr. Jackson. "Now, Clint, I have a proposition for you. I've been a part of an ongoing discussion with members of the mayor's office and the local chamber of commerce related to workforce development for our city. We're trying to be intentional about bringing high-potential leaders and professionals back to town after they've received an education in colleges around the country. It's important for our community not to lose the good ones. And you, Clint, are one of the good ones. I know you have a year of school left and have pictured yourself working in the big city. But would you ever consider coming back to Grace Harbor after graduation?"

Clint, eyes wide, simply looked at Dr. Jackson. He felt a slight flush creep up his neck.

"I could see you being a core leader here one day, furthering our mission for the next generation," Dr. Jackson said for his closing argument.

Clint was taken aback. He had never considered this path for his future. Feeling humbled, uncertain, and a bit overwhelmed, he looked at his mentor and said, "Do I have to decide today, or can I take a few days to think about it? I mean, Esther took a few days to fast and pray, didn't she?"

Dr. Jackson grinned again and replied, "I wouldn't want you to decide today, nor would I want you to decide without praying about it. We can stay in touch over the next few months while you're back in school and talk it through later." He stood and extended a hand to his young intern. Clint accepted the handshake.

"No matter what path you choose," said Dr. Jackson, "I'm proud of you. Lead from the Core, and God will continue to use you, just like he has this summer."

Clint felt his eyes well up. "Thank you, sir," he said, a firm grasp still on Dr. Jackson's hand. "I can't say it enough. Thank you."

The Stories That People Tell about You

As Tom Kinsey concluded his speech, the room erupted with applause. The emcee came to the podium and brought the next speaker, the mayor, to the stage.

The mayor referenced the same program Dr. Jackson had pitched to Clint on his last day of the internship. She credited Grace Harbor and Dr. Jackson for being the model for developing the next generation of leaders, not only in their city but in the entire state. She also mentioned several statistics related to workforce development. One of those "statistics" was sitting next to his wife, Kristen, elbows leaning on his knees, hands clasped and placed under his chin.

Clint was amazed at how much had happened since his college graduation over twenty years before. What had started as a "plan B" internship had become an integral part of his life and purpose. He remembered making a call to Dr. Jackson in January of his senior year in college. "Dr. Jackson," Clint began, "I did it—I asked Kristen to marry me! And can you believe she said yes?"

"I sure can, Clint. That's great! I can't wait to hear all about it," replied the proud mentor.

"I have a few minutes before class, and I wanted to ask you a couple of quick questions. First, would you be willing to perform our wedding ceremony next summer? And second, are you still interested in me coming to work at Grace Harbor?"

Dr. Jackson, his eyes a bit misty, said, "Yes, of course—on both accounts."

Clint and Kristen Smith moved to Clint's hometown the summer after their wedding and began their life together. Clint also started his career as an entry-level employee in the finance and operations department at Grace Harbor. His role was not glamorous, working in a small office in a forgotten hallway. He was a long way from his dreams of having a downtown view in a big-city corporate office building. But even on the hard days, Clint found his work to be rewarding.

Over the first few years of his career, Clint and Dr. Jackson remained in touch, continuing their mentoring relationship. While many knew Clint's story—the local boy who had been hand-selected by the CEO to become a summer intern—both he and Dr. Jackson knew it was best that Clint earn respect and responsibility through his own actions.

Clint's focus on the leadership Core, combined with his natural emotional intelligence and his focus on people, allowed him to rise quickly at Grace Harbor. When he was only in his early thirties, he was named the youngest vice president in the company's history. His next major milestone was becoming the chief operating officer of

Grace Harbor, allowing him to work closer than ever with his mentor and friend, Dr. Bill Jackson.

From conversations in the hallway to senior leadership meetings, Clint observed Dr. Jackson repeatedly point his team to the leadership Core. Hardly a week passed without Dr. Jackson referencing the story of Esther and Mordecai. They might as well have been team members at Grace Harbor! Clint enjoyed his front-row seat watching the CEO lead. The hospital had never been on such solid footing financially. The team was robust, and the outlook was positive.

While Dr. Jackson's grin was still present, Clint had noticed a shift in his leader's energy and focus. He was less caught up in Grace Harbor's present and more concerned with its future. Dr. Jackson regularly spoke to his wife, closest friends, and colleagues, including his mentee Clint, of his career timeline and the need to start planning for a leadership transition. The Grace Harbor board of directors wasn't ready to see him leave. They suggested he extend his contract, arguing that only Dr. Jackson, as the CEO, could see them through an upcoming capital expansion campaign.

Dr. Jackson relented and signed a new contract, but only under the condition that the board would craft a succession plan. He also decided he would not be a part of hiring his replacement, other than meeting with the finalists near the end of the search. Leading from the Core, he wanted his successor to know he had been chosen by the people, not by the outgoing CEO. With the new plan in place and many of his daily duties delegated to others, Dr. Jackson felt as though the fog had lifted, giving him a clear vision of the finish line.

One day, about six months before the retirement banquet, Dr. Jackson asked Clint to stay behind after a leadership team meeting.

As Dr. Jackson closed the door to his office, Clint sat down in his customary spot at the small circular table.

"Clint," Dr. Jackson began, "are you doing okay? You seem to be a bit caught up in the fog."

"You know, I could probably use a little fog-cutting today."

"Well, let's get it out there and talk it over," said Dr. Jackson.

"There's just a lot going on right now," Clint explained. "The campaign is going well, and my team is doing great work, but I can't quit thinking about your transition as CEO. I'm having a really hard time picturing myself working for someone other than you. Few CEOs see leadership through the same Core lens as you. When I talk to my friends at other hospitals around the country—even those that are faith-based like Grace Harbor—they often share horror stories of what their bosses are like. Many are miserable. I guess I'm nervous that your successor will change this place. One of my greatest fears is that we don't have what it takes to carry on. We can't all be you."

With kindness in his eyes, Dr. Jackson said, "Clint, you and your colleagues have done a tremendous job leading your teams. I'm not just saying that to make you feel good—I hear it from your team! Your example of humble leadership inspires them. From what they're telling me, they'd follow you anywhere. Do you remember what your leadership brand is?"

"Yes—your leadership brand is made up of the stories people tell about you."

"That's right. Clint, your followers are telling some very good stories about you."

"That's nice of you to say, Dr. Jackson," said Clint, wiping a rogue tear from his eye. "My people are the best. I care a lot about them."

"Of course you do, Clint. You work for their good and speak up for their welfare consistently, and they appreciate you for it. Regarding your other comment, the one you said a moment ago about not everyone being like me, we need to address that too. Clint, I started sharing about the leadership Core with you not so you could be like me but so you could be a better you. It's each leader's responsibility to develop and lead from the Core. If you're not authentic to yourself, you'll never be as influential as you could be. God entrusted you with talents, gifts, and training that only you can steward. If you don't rise to the occasion, who will? Do you remember our first summer together, the first of many times I told you about Esther?"

"Of course," said Clint. "It changed my life."

Dr. Jackson grinned. "There's a character in the story who is never explicitly mentioned. It's an interesting literary device because he's the *main* character. Can you guess who it is?"

Clint thought for a moment before answering, "Is it the classic Sunday school answer? God?"

"Bingo!" said Dr. Jackson. "The name of God never comes up, but that doesn't mean he's not at work. The book of Esther is full of leadership lessons. But beyond that, we see a bigger story unfolding—God's plan for the lives of those who are willing to let him use them. Your future at Grace Harbor is solid, not because of my role as CEO, but because you are consistently seeking to do God's will. He will not forsake you. With his help, you will be a leader wherever you are, no matter who is running this hospital."

Clint, appreciative of his mentor's ability to continually help him see the big picture, said, "Thanks, Dr. Jackson. I needed to be reminded of that truth."

He fell quiet for a moment before his mentor asked, "Is there anything else on your mind, Clint?"

"Well," Clint began, "I've been approached about a significant leadership opportunity—a possible new role. And I've struggled to make a decision. I don't know if I'm worthy or prepared for such an opportunity."

"I'm happy to help you process this opportunity, Clint. But no matter what path you take, if you go in and focus on leading from the Core, with a sincere desire to work for the good of the people and speak up for their welfare, that organization will benefit from having you lead them. I encourage you to pray and reflect. And no matter which path you take, make sure you know where you're going—and why."

Clint looked his mentor in the eyes and said, "Thank you for your time today, and really, over all the years. Learning about the Core has led me to this moment. Without your mentorship, I wouldn't even be considered for this opportunity. For that, I will be forever grateful, no matter how things turn out."

With that, Clint got up, gave his mentor a hug, shook his hand, and walked out. He returned to his office, picked up his cell phone, and made a call: "Good afternoon, this is Clint Smith. I'm returning your call about the position we've discussed recently. It's with a great sense of humility that I would like to officially submit my name for consideration for the position."

CHAPTER 13

A Farewell Speech

As the mayor wrapped up her presentation and the crowd applauded, it dawned on Clint that the evening was drawing to a close. The only agenda item left was Dr. Jackson's speech. Clint took a sip of his now-lukewarm coffee, realizing that tears were forming in his eyes.

Clint touched his wife on her shoulder. Kristen turned to him and saw the look on his face. This was a sacred moment, marking the end of one of the most meaningful eras of her husband's life. She took his hand and squeezed it gently. The emcee's voice filled the room: "Please join me in welcoming to the podium our leader, our friend, and the person we are here to say thank you to for three decades of service to Grace Harbor Regional Hospital—ladies and gentlemen, Dr. Bill Jackson!"

Clint and Kristen stood and clapped. Clint glanced at the crowd of adoring faces, all here to celebrate the man who was now making his way to the stage. The room was full of Grace Harbor employees, from executive board members to the janitorial staff. CEOs and leaders from across the region were present. Former patients, community leaders, and church friends were scattered throughout the crowd. All had gathered to give honor and say thanks to someone who had truly led them toward better lives.

Clint didn't even try to hold the tears back as he found his seat. Upon arriving at the podium, Dr. Jackson asked his wife, June, to join him so she could be acknowledged for the role she'd played throughout the years. Kristen looked back at Clint and smiled.

Dr. Jackson looked at his speech notes for a moment, then folded them up and put them into his suit coat pocket. As Clint had suspected, his mentor was about to go "off script." Dr. Jackson began by telling the audience that he was extremely humbled they had taken the time to be there that evening. He then apologized that ice cream was not being served for dessert.

After a hearty laugh, the room fell silent. Dr. Jackson was quiet for a moment, made eye contact with his wife, and cleared his throat before beginning: "I would like to tell you a story. The main characters are named Haman, Esther, and Mordecai. And they will teach us about the Core of leadership."

Those sitting at Clint's table looked at him and mouthed, "How did you know he would speak about this?" Clint smiled back and whispered, "I just had a feeling!"

For the next twenty-five minutes, Dr. Jackson told the story Clint had heard hundreds of times. For many in the room, it was their first time hearing how Haman had an ego out of control, and how Esther embraced the truth and led with courage. They learned of a guy named Mordecai, who worked hard for the good of the people and regularly spoke up for their welfare.

Dr. Jackson concluded his speech by reminding the audience: "Leadership is for everyone. No matter your role or title, leaders are those who work for the good of the people and speak up for their welfare." After concluding his final speech as CEO of Grace Harbor, he made his way back to his wife's side as the entire room stood and gave him thunderous applause.

As everyone in attendance gathered their things to leave, one of the women sitting at Clint's table said, "He's such a great man. I'm sure you learned a lot working with him over the years, Clint."

A man at the table chimed in, "Dr. Jackson may be retiring soon, but I think he's got another career in speaking ahead of him!"

Clint agreed with everyone and wished them all well. As he and Kristen moved through the crowd toward the exit, he looked back at the head table where Dr. Jackson, still smiling and hugging those crowded around him, noticed his mentee.

Dr. Jackson made a fist and, placing it against his body, began to pat his core.

Clint made a fist and did the same.

The Next Chapter

Two weeks later, on the first Monday of the new month, Clint hurried across the vacant parking lot from his parking spot in the back. Eager to start his first day in his new role, he'd arrived early so he could get a few things done before making the rounds in the hospital. His first order of business would be to introduce himself to the people he was called to lead.

Sitting down at his new desk, he opened a drawer and found a notepad on which to write his to-do list. A beautifully wrapped box caught his attention. How had it gotten into his desk drawer? He took out the gift, which was labeled: *To Clint Smith, Chief Executive Officer.*

Smiling, Clint opened the package and found a brown leather Bible with his name monogrammed on the front cover. A piece of paper was sticking out from the pages. He opened the makeshift bookmark to the tenth chapter of the book of Esther, where he noticed that the third verse was brightly highlighted: "Mordecai the Jew was second in rank to King Xerxes, preeminent among the Jews, and held in high esteem by his many fellow Jews, because he worked for the good of his people and spoke up for the welfare of all the Jews."

Clint smiled. The gift giver was no longer a mystery.

He went on to read the handwritten note:

Dear Clint,

I'm so proud of you and look forward to seeing what you do in your new role. Contained in this Bible are so many lessons that will help you as you lead into the future. I've marked a few of my favorites and hope you will add to them as you go along. Remember to keep the Leadership Core at the forefront as you serve the people you have been entrusted with leading.

God bless,

Bill

P.S. When the days as the CEO of Grace Harbor are challenging and you need someone to talk to, I know a great little hole-in-the-wall where we can meet for lunch.

Clint held the Bible to his chest for a moment before setting it down. He picked up his pen and wrote out his first week's to-do list:

Lead from the Core
Work for the Good of the People
- Walk around and visit team members in their offices
- Write birthday cards for Grace Harbor staff members
- Hire an intern for the summer

Keep Your Ego in Check
- Park away from the building and walk

- Sign up for a slot in the Grace Harbor community service project

Embrace Truth
- Develop three good questions to ask at employee town hall meetings
- Prepare response to patient surveys

Lead with Your Ears
- Be an active listener
- Talk to those on the front lines

Show Up with Grace
- Show up early to employee going-away party and talk to their family members
- Have an up-front conversation with an employee who isn't performing to their potential

Pace Yourself and Extend the Game
- Schedule date night with Kristen
- Attend men's Bible study on Saturday
- Take the kids for ice cream after their concert

Be Coachable
- Participate in leadership small group
- Complete personal assessment

Know Where You're Going and Why
- Remember my "why"
- Provide clarity and connection for all to our mission and vision

The Leadership Core

15. Work for the good of the people.
16. Keep your ego in check.
17. Embrace truth.
18. Lead with your ears.
19. Show up with grace.
20. Pace yourself and extend the game.
21. Be coachable.
22. Know where you're going and why.

From Story to Application

You've just read the story of Dr. Jackson and Clint—a real-life example of what it looks like to lead from the Core. To be clear, the story wasn't a retelling of our friendship, though it was inspired by road trips and conversations we've shared. As you'll discover in part two of the book, it's a patchwork of real experiences, time-tested ideas, and hard-earned wisdom.

Unlike many other leadership paradigms, the leadership Core isn't just for CEOs or corporate executives. It's for everyone. It's for school principals navigating burnout among teachers. For nonprofit leaders trying to do more with less. For young parents in the throes of raising toddlers. For blue-collar managers juggling priorities. For small-business owners, faith leaders, rising stars, and anyone responsible for helping others move forward.

Leadership is not a clean formula. It's messy, unpredictable, and deeply personal. But despite the chaos, there are core truths that can anchor us, principles that hold steady in the swirl of deadlines, decisions, and difficult conversations.

That's why we're shifting gears from story to strategy. It's one thing to know about leadership—it's another to do it. You wouldn't want to fly with a pilot who has only read the manual and watched a few videos. You want someone who has logged hours in the cockpit! The same is true for leadership: It's forged in real-world experience, not just theory.

The Leadership Core principles are biblical, but they've also proven effective in secular organizations. We've seen them work in churches, boardrooms, classrooms, and construction sites.

And with that, let's get ready to lead from the Core.

Work for the Good of the People

It perhaps seems strange that with all the lectures, seminars, and books on leadership currently available, we would begin this section of the book by asking the question "What is leadership?" John Maxwell is famous for defining leadership with one word: *influence.* Peter Drucker said, "The only definition of a leader is someone who has followers." Kevin Cashman suggested that leadership is "authentic influence that creates value." Margaret Wheatley described leadership as "a series of behaviors rather than a role for heroes." Sheryl Sandberg suggests, "Leadership is about making others better as a result of your presence and making sure that impact lasts in your absence." Others say leadership is simply moving people or an organization of people from one point to another. Some have used words such as *governance, administration, control,* or *power* to describe it.

Leadership is not easy to define. It's a bit like *love, joy,* or *happiness*. We have a sense of what the words mean, but a precise definition often escapes us. However, we generally know good leadership when we see it, and we certainly know it when we *don't* see it.

The definition of leadership I (Ken) will propose is the very best I have ever heard. It is not only a definition but also serves as a depiction—or picture—of what takes place within the act of leading. This depiction will change your entire view of who you really are as a leader. Where did I find it? Quite by accident. One day, I was sitting in a Bible class at church. The teacher was ending his comments on the book of Esther. As he talked, I glanced at what was written at the end of Esther, and I happened to read—*really* read—the last verse of the book.

There it was. The best definition of leadership I had ever read.

As we learned earlier from Dr. Jackson, the words come at the end of the book when describing how Mordecai was "held in high esteem by his many fellow Jews, because *he worked for the good of his people* and spoke up for the welfare of all the Jews" (Esther 10:3, emphasis added).

That is the best description of leadership I've ever heard. Leaders are about the business of *working for the good of the people they lead*. That's it—that's all there is to it. Leading is not about the welfare of the leader; it's about the welfare of those being led!

Presidents, CEOs, ministers, department heads, supervisors, even spouses and parents have one job, and that job is to work for the good of the people they lead.

If asked the question, "Who do you work for?" what would be your response?

I work for the board of directors. I work for the president. I work for my principal.

These answers might sound right, but they're actually the wrong idea. Leaders don't look *up* the org chart to see for whom they work. They look *down* the org chart to see for whom they work. The better you serve those who follow you, the better you'll be able to lead. And the better you lead, the better the organization, the better the profits, the better the morale—the better *everything* will be!

A Leader's View of People

The very first step in working for the good of your people is to get to know them. Many of us can relate to the experience of having a boss who didn't seem to truly know us. They failed to recognize the unique nature and giftings that you or your colleagues possessed.

Why is this?

One reason is that for far too long, people in leadership roles have operated more like managers than leaders. They may mean well, but often they're more consumed with doing things well and being timely, so hyper-focused on structure, rules, or procedures that they fail to be personable and vulnerable enough to build the relationships necessary to influence others and achieve results.

Let me paint a picture with an example from my organizational consulting experience. A new CEO assumed the role of leadership at an organization where their predecessor had led with a strong desire for growth at all costs, valued new ideas and attention-grabbing headlines, and exhibited little regard for strategic planning, policies, and structure. The board had heard the employee base's cries for a new

CEO who could provide more order, stronger policies, and a renewed commitment to organizational structure and discipline.

The new CEO was well suited for their role, as it was apparent from day one they were going to be intentional and calculating about planning, creating new rules and procedures, and sticking to the agenda.

While many in the organization had hoped for a move away from the "Wild Wild West" approach of the previous leadership, they weren't ready for the whiplash the new leader's operating style would create. Whereas meetings had once been full of opportunities to share one's dreams about a topic or project, discuss how one's family was doing, or talk about one's career trajectory, they now consisted of agendas timed down to the minute where each topic of conversation was structured and anyone who strayed from the subject at hand was corrected on spot.

One-on-one meetings with the new CEO often started with the announcement of how many minutes were available to meet, and only rarely did they include any questions or discussion related to life outside of work. Performance reviews that had once included conversations about the career aspirations of the team members involved were replaced with a robust set of questions and responses that were so mechanical and structured, they left no time or space for anything other than a review of the tactical components of one's role.

After a few years, the constant focus on rules, order, structure, and policy, combined with a lack of attention to anything else that might normally be connected to building relationships, had created an environment where the CEO was seen as unapproachable and completely transactional. Team members often referred to their boss as a "robot" or "machine."

People across the organization started noticing how things were being handled, and word spread like wildfire that the new CEO didn't care at all about the people they were leading. This was not entirely true, as the CEO did care; they just didn't seem to be able to naturally move from an approach that felt transactional to one that was more relational. The adage about perception preceding facts rang true across the organization, and it didn't take long for employee retention and morale to decline significantly.

Here's the lesson: Effective leadership is not about styles and strategies. It's about *people*.

People are the foremost asset of leaders. People have the creativity, genius, talent, drive, work ethic, and power to make dreams come true. Well-led people can change the world. Poorly led people, at best, maintain the status quo, and, at worst, tear organizations apart.

People are the single most important item that separates managers from leaders. Management is about control, with managers controlling time, budgets, and anything else that can be controlled. Every leader will do some managing, but real leadership goes beyond management of things to trust and empowerment of people.

The real question now arises: *How* does a leader go about knowing and empowering their people? Because people are complex, leading them requires wisdom. What follows are six "People Principles" I have observed and applied over decades of leadership. As with all other Leadership Core principles, these principles are incredibly simple. Yet, when combined and placed within the portfolio of a leader's basic belief system, they contribute to great leadership, allowing every leader to work for the good of their people.

People Principle #1: Every Person Is Different

More than a billion people live on this earth, and every one of them is different from all the others.

It's reasonable to assume that many of you who are reading this book not only have siblings but, along with your siblings, grew up with the same parents, the same house, the same extended family, and the same traditions. But if someone asked if you and your siblings are different from each other, the answer would return as a very loud "Yes!" From how we dress, to what time we prefer to get up in the morning, to how we feel about life issues, to predominant moods, we are profoundly different from each other.

All the excitement and attention you were given on the day you were born is nothing in comparison to the joy and thrill your Creator feels. He already knows you. In fact, he already knows the unique set of gifts, strengths, talents, and abilities that are within each of us from the beginning. He sees us as individuals, specially made to fulfill a "me-sized" gap on earth.

Fortunes have been made by those who develop and deliver personality profiles and assessments. I think I have taken them all and can tell you that whatever number, series of letters, color, animal, or genius that each assessment uses to describe me, I learn a little more about the particular and unique nature of who I was created to be. I am different, and so are you. And as leaders, we should never forget the power that comes from our people's differences.

A leader understands there is power in being different. Individual differences are what make teams so valuable. Everyone has a unique contribution to offer. Each person brings their own view, talents, and energy to the task at hand. For the most important things in life, it's not more bodies doing the same thing that makes big dreams come true; rather, it's a team of unique individuals making a wholehearted contribution that turns the greatest of dreams into reality.

For an organization to work effectively, there's no way around unilateral decision-making. Yet great leaders are aware that not everyone will receive the decision in the same way. What one follower likes, another will dislike. What works well for one person doesn't necessarily work well for another. This awareness may not change the decision, but it can change the way the decision is made and delivered. Followers can sense when a leader has made a decision with the awareness that every person is unique. They can also feel the leader's empathy and understanding that factor into the decision, which is a result of the leader embracing this Core principle.

People Principle #2: Every Person Is the Same

Though every person is different, if you pull back the layers and reach the core of each of us, we're all relatively the same. If a group of ten people assembled and one person was asked to describe how it felt to be discouraged or rejected, would you not think that the story of the one would mirror almost exactly the story the other nine would tell? When it comes to deep, personal issues, we are all very similar.

As I write this, two of my friends within the last two months have been diagnosed with cancer. One two months ago, the other yesterday. They have different occupations—one is a successful real estate developer, the other a commercial airline pilot. In fact, they are different in almost every way, yet they're the same in this core issue—in a situation that is so deeply personal. Both would describe the shock, fear, and concern about their diagnosis in exactly the same way. Suz (my wife) and I know how they feel. Several years ago, we received the diagnosis that she had breast cancer. Our story of shock, fear, and concern is identical to the stories of my two friends.

In certain issues, leaders can predict with near certainty how followers will respond and react because of how similar we all are. When a leader approaches people with this deeply embedded awareness, followers don't just sense empathy and understanding—they see it and feel it from the leader.

And that kind of leadership—the kind that's rooted not in position but in shared humanity—is what draws people close. When a leader understands that beneath our varied roles and personalities lie the same fears, longings, and vulnerabilities, they lead not from a distance but from alongside. It's not charisma that connects us in moments of crisis but compassion. And it's not strategy that steadies us but the steady presence of someone who simply understands.

People Principle #3: Every Person Is Smart

Over my forty years of being in the leadership and people business, I have learned that every person is smart. I don't necessarily mean smart in all ways or smart in the same ways—in fact, some of us can be very lacking (or dumb) at times—but every person is still very smart. I never cease to be amazed at the individual, God-given talents of people.

One of the significant loves of my life is my ranch. It is a working cattle operation, which involves some farming. Our son, Mitch, manages the ranch and does the everyday hard work on it while I get to enjoy it as a wonderful escape from daily routines.

Several years ago, my son became acquainted with a man named Bob. Bob and his wife carried tools from place to place to do odd jobs. Because Mitch and I have little ability to do mechanical tasks, we often called upon Bob to help us. After months of employing Bob for odd jobs, Mitch mentioned it would be nice if we had a place on one of our farms where Bob could live and work for us on a more full-time basis. I suggested an area where a manufactured home sat at one time. It had a storm cellar, working plumbing, and a shop for all of Bob's tools.

Mitch asked Bob if he would like to join us on the ranch. His response was an immediate "yes." I gave Bob the budget for a new manufactured home and told him to see what he could find. It wasn't long before he had located one. In a short time, the home was purchased, moved, and set in place. It didn't look like much to me, but after Bob did some work on it, including replacing the windows and flooring, he transformed it into the perfect home for him.

Today, Bob is an important part of our daily operations on the ranch. In fact, I've often said I don't know what we would do without him. I have a PhD in engineering, and Bob never finished high school. Yet, working beside him, I am reminded again and again of how smart he is as he constantly repairs and fixes things and operates various machinery and tools. I frequently ask myself the question: *In this environment, which one of us is the smartest?*

Can you guess my answer?

Bob, of course.

Unfortunately, far too many people who hold leadership positions take the approach that they must be seen as the smartest person in the room. Often, these "leaders" will diminish the abilities, beliefs, and expertise of others on the team to prop themselves up.

I (Matt) once heard a dramatic example of this from a higher education consultant. Decades ago while he was serving as a vice president and member of the leadership team at a university, a new president came on board. At their first team meeting, the president went around the conference room table and looked every cabinet member in the eyes, declaring that, if he had to, he could do each of their jobs better than they could. My friend was stunned. Everyone in the room had been immediately sized up and judged, and they walked away knowing where they "ranked" with their new leader.

While most people don't experience such blunt-force trauma, chances are they have similar stories to tell. We've all felt less than or marginalized by a "leader." It isn't pretty, and it doesn't lead to positive results. However, when leaders recognize the giftedness and unique perspectives of those around them and are willing to empower their people, a new level of trust is formed. And trust is imperative between leaders and their followers if an organization is to become all it can be.

People Principle #4: Every Person Is Important

Many years ago, I (Ken) was asked to deliver a series of sermons in a small, rural church over the course of several evenings. Speeches were to be given on Sunday and then on Monday and Tuesday evenings, and they had plans to invite their entire community to be a part of the series. I remember arriving early on a Sunday morning, as is my habit. As I walked up to the white porch of this small building, I was surprised to see three men waiting there to meet me.

Two of the men were very short in stature. The third man introduced himself and then introduced the other two, John and Glen. I later learned that Glen had developed some kind of chemical deficiency before he was born, which left him with physical and intellectual disabilities. John had Down syndrome.

After we were introduced to each other, John began to speak so rapidly that I could hardly understand a word. The third gentleman told me John's dream was to be a preacher. Standing there with a huge Bible tucked under his arm, John was all smiles as that message was relayed to me. A little while later, I walked into the auditorium, and there was John on the stage, walking back and forth, waving his arms. He was playing the role of a preacher.

Late that Sunday evening, I drove three hours back to my home, ready to get some good rest before returning to the church the following evening. I told Suz and our two children about John and how he could read a bit from that huge Bible. Someone had the idea for me to give him a new, modern-language version of the Bible, which I did on Monday night. John was thrilled. He kept coming up to me, waving the Bible, and saying, "Thank you, buddy!"

On Tuesday evening, when the event was over, I was in the lobby talking to people. I saw an elderly woman standing next to John and Glen. After I learned that John was her son, she walked up to me and said some words I hope I never forget: "I want to thank you for giving John the Bible." Then, looking over at the two men, she said, "You know, they are people too."

Yes, these were the words of a mother, but they were also words of great truth. John's mother was telling me that they—John and Glen—were important people. As a leader, the essence of that story never gets far from me. Every individual is very important and should be treated as such.

People not only should be treated as though they are important, but they should also be frequently *told* they are important. Employees need to know the answer to several basic questions: Where are we going? Can I trust the one who is leading me to that place? And am I an important part of the journey?

Every person needs to hear that they are important to the greater mission. Each member of your team needs to know their own talents, gifts, and abilities are valuable and unique. They need to feel they are special and that they are key to the achievement of the overall goals and impact of your organization. As you reflect on this, maybe ask yourself the following question: When was the last time I told them just how important they are?

People Principle #5: Everyone Has a Story

Our lives are a story we write each day. If we don't like the story, we can change it at any moment. Your story, like mine, is unique. And you, like me, can tell your story at a moment's notice, pouring it out from the depths of your heart.

Most people, given the right environment, want to tell their story, to share and connect with others. When someone intently and sincerely listens to me tell my story, I feel valued and important. My story might make you laugh, cry, reflect, light up, feel happy, or become sad. Whatever the emotion it produces, when I see its effect on you, I feel seen and valued.

Leaders aren't supposed to spend the majority of their time doing routine management tasks. Instead, they should be spending much of their time working for the good of the people. And what better way to accomplish this than to take the time to listen to a person's story?

Listening to others takes time. Depending on the size of the organization, it could take years. Great leaders are willing to invest that time. Slowly, they work their way through the organization, pausing and asking individuals from all areas, "Would you tell me your story?"

The more stories you hear as a leader, the healthier the organization will be. Yes, it's important to get work done, and every meeting needs an agenda and direction. But it's also extremely important to be relational in your workplace, and there may be no better way to engage with those you lead than by listening to their stories.

It will do wonders for your leadership and for the people in your care if you know the names of your employees' kids and ask how they are doing. Or if you meet with your direct reports in their offices and ask questions about the pictures they display on their bookshelves. Or if you show real interest in the vacation they just returned from.

Be a real person with your people. Remember, you are there to work for the good of these people, so you should know who you are working for.

Because we all are writing a new page to our story every day, if a leader knows the story, they can, at times, help others write a better next page or next chapter. It is the most important, personal step a leader can take in the development of the people they lead. Pause and think of those in your life who actively and purposefully helped *you* write a new and better chapter to your life. How do you feel about them? Are you grateful for them? Do you trust them? Are they someone you admire? Do you care about them?

If that's how you want people to feel about you, then spend time listening to their stories and devoting yourself to building an environment for them to write a better next page. As a leader, you must be willing to help your people write the story they dream of writing about their lives.

People Principle #6: Everyone Needs Encouragement

It could be argued that this is the most important principle of all. In some ways, it encompasses all the others. Encouragement is the act of putting courage in the hearts of people. One of my favorite examples of this is found in the book of Job where it says, "Your words have supported those who stumbled; you have strengthened faltering knees" (4:4). I personally love to summarize that passage in the following way, "Your words have kept men on their feet." Did you know that encouragement can be given without words? It can be shared with a nod, a smile, a pat on the back, a helping hand, a gift, or simply the act of standing silently beside someone. But by far the greatest method of encouragement is one's words. Never forget that your words can keep people on their feet, or that they can knock them over. Your words have power.

The words you share, whether during a time of organizational or personal crisis or just in an ordinary hallway conversation, can make a difference in the day, week, month, career, or life of someone who looks to you for guidance.

As wonderful as life is, it is also very, very difficult. No person goes through life without experiencing obstacles. Thankfully, most of them are small, but small problems can accumulate to make life difficult. Large obstacles may not be as frequent, but they arrive with such strength and force that we wonder if we can survive them. And when the weight of this difficult life becomes so heavy that our knees begin to falter, our steps grow weak, and our pace grows still, words of encouragement can be what keeps us going.

When you're discouraged, nothing seems exciting. Energy is weak. Negative thoughts pile one upon another. You don't feel like being around people. You'd prefer to withdraw and hide. You feel sorry for yourself. You feel alone and helpless. I'm speaking from personal experience, but does this sound familiar? I'm certain your answer is *yes*. Experiencing times of discouragement is one of those ways in which we are all the same.

Like everyone else, I need encouragement. Thankfully, my wife has been excellent at giving it to me. My entire family has been encouraging at the times when I needed it. Often, encouragement has come from a person whose name I don't even know. Their words kept me on my feet during a difficult time.

For the last thirty years, I have given a lot of speeches. I know what it's like to give a good speech, and painfully, I know what it's like to give a not-so-good speech. I've arrived at the point where I can tell shortly into the speech which way it's going to go.

Long before I've finished a speech, I can see and feel the response of the audience. If my wife is in the audience and I return to my seat beside her, when I think no one is looking, I will lean over and ask how it went, despite the fact that I already know the answer. So, why do I ask her? Because *I need encouragement.*

That's the truth about me, you, and everyone else—we all need encouragement. My wife needs it. My children need it, no matter their age. My grandchildren need it. My friends need it. My coworkers need it. People who are led by me need it. I have found that even nameless strangers I meet along the way need it.

It's so easy to share a word of encouragement with others. You can pause while walking into your office and tell the person doing the landscaping what a great job they're doing. You can say to a coworker, "I don't know what I'd do without you." I have the opportunity to speak at many events and my role is the easy part. I get to walk in and say hello to those that have gathered and deliver a speech. I try so very hard to always make sure to thank the countless people who work so hard behind the scenes to make those opportunities special and bring people together. You can show appreciation for the little things people do, by sending a thank-you card or email, or just by walking over to someone's desk and saying thanks. It does not have to be a big or showy thank you.

Some outstanding leaders have dedicated themselves to being encouraging to their team members by practicing the art of showing up during life's ups and downs. Followers often remember when their leader came to the funeral home after the loss of a loved one or sent a wedding present or a birthday card. People want to know you care for them as an individual, and you can demonstrate this by being an encourager.

Yet if giving encouragement is so easy, why do so many of us fail at it?

There's a multitude of reasons. Some of us are just a bit too self-centered to think about others. Some of us are "too busy." But being busy is not the badge of honor our culture makes it out to be. Busyness is robbing us of some of our most important treasures. It is certainly robbing leaders of the use of one of their most powerful leadership tools—encouragement. You cannot encourage unless you are aware, and you cannot be aware unless you stop running from one thing to the next and take the time to actually *see* people. When you slow down enough to become aware of others' hopes and hurts, you can share the encouragement that helps keep them on their feet.

Leaders are givers of hope. Leaders speak words of optimism. Leaders cast visions of a greater tomorrow. Most of all, leaders see people right where they are and encourage them.

Work for the Good of Your People

Mordecai's example teaches us that leadership is not a title we wear but a responsibility we bear. Each of us has been given the responsibility to know, value, and encourage those entrusted to our care.

How you view people lies at the core of your ability to influence them. People are your most important asset. Leaders, therefore, are stewards of people as much as they are stewards of money or facilities. I would argue that a leader has far greater responsibility for people than for any facility or financial asset. Without the people, everything else will likely prove to be meaningless.

So, work for the good of your people. Speak up for their welfare. Give them encouragement. It is the essence of the leadership

Core. While each of these principles are connected, this one is at the center of it all. Leadership is not about me. It is about elevating and stewarding those we have been entrusted to lead. Choosing to focus on others will be the single greatest decision you can make as a leader.

Keep Your Ego in Check

Growing up in West Texas, we didn't have a lot of opportunities for water-focused recreational activities. When I (Matt) was around twelve years old, my friend's dad offered to take a small group of us to the lake to learn how to water ski and ride an inner tube. I'm not naturally an adrenaline junkie, but when you're twelve and your friends are excited about something, you naturally get excited about it too.

Out on the lake, I watched my friends take turns riding the inner tube. They made it look so easy. I mean, how hard could it be? You just lie there on the tube, hold on, and don't let go. *No problem*, I thought to myself when it was my turn to hop into the water, collect the rope handles, and then climb aboard the tube. My plan was to take it nice and easy and hang on until it felt like I'd done enough to punch my twelve-year-old "adrenaline-junkie card" and then allow someone else to have a turn.

I was trying to remember the instructions my friend's dad had given me when all of a sudden, I heard the engine roar. I was quickly thrust out of the water and started bouncing around on the tube. It felt like we were speeding along at one hundred miles an hour, but it probably was closer to ten. As we drove straight ahead, I found myself enjoying the smooth ride in the middle of the boat's wake.

The lake wasn't large, and as my friend's dad made the first turn, I encountered a new reality I hadn't considered before: sliding outside the wake. The smooth path I'd been riding along on was now bumpier and harder to handle. My skinny twelve-year-old arms were straining to hold on to the handle as I rode the rough water outside the wake. Proud that I was surviving this challenge, I began to wonder if I was destined to be a professional inner tube rider.

Then the boat's path straightened again, and I returned to the middle of the wake. A moment later, I encountered another challenge: a jet skier jumping the waves of the boat's wake was getting a little too close for comfort.

My friend's dad was being extremely careful with us that day. He was worried that I might let go of the handles at a bad time, and if the jet skier wasn't paying attention, it could be a problem. He sped up a little and made a turn so he could get me safely to another part of the lake, away from the jet skier.

Unfortunately, the jet skier didn't take the hint and kept coming closer. My friend's dad decided to turn again quickly, and I was flung back and forth over the wake. On one of the turns, I slid outside the wake and crashed into a floating buoy, catapulting my ninety-five-pound self what felt like hundreds of feet into the air before I landed safely in the calm waters below.

As my friend's dad directed a few choice words toward the jet skier about safety and children, I remember the look of awe on my friends' faces as I, a conquering hero, stepped back onto the boat, having successfully navigated the unpredictable twists and turns of my adventure.

The Leadership Wake

Dr. Henry Cloud uses the term "leadership wake" to describe the effect a leader has on their environment. As they move their organization ahead, they leave a trail, just as a boat cutting through the water creates a wake. Their influence creates waves, impacting relationships and results.

All leaders leave a wake for their followers. Sometimes the wake is smooth and peaceful. At other times it's a little chaotic and exciting. And then there are the times when it takes all you have to hold on.

The second Core leadership principle is to keep your ego in check, because an ego out of control is destined to leave a wake of destruction. As we saw in the story of Esther, Haman left behind chaos, destruction, and even death threats in his wake. His pride was out of control, making it difficult and dangerous for people to follow him.

To state this principle in the opposite form, humility is a Core leadership virtue. Jim Collins's work from many years ago, *From Good to Great*, is based on the premise that effective leaders must be humble. He highlights many great companies that were led by people who prioritized humility. In his next book, *How the Mighty Fall*, Collins explains how his research found that the number one reason organizations fail was inordinate pride. All too often leaders begin to believe they are the reason for the successes an organization may have. Collins stated, "Those who fail to acknowledge the role luck may have played in their success—and thereby overestimate their own merit and capabilities—have succumbed to hubris," and hubris, he suggests, is "excessive pride that brings down a hero, or alternatively, outrageous arrogance that inflicts suffering upon the innocent." As we seek to lead from the Core, we must leave the excessive hubris behind and lean more fully into a leadership stance based on humility.

A Nation of Narcissists

Haman, whom you learned about in part one, would have loved living in the age of TikTok. Psychologist Jean Twenge and many others have noted that we live in an age of narcissism. In nearly every industry, it's easy to find people in "leadership" roles who seem more consumed with themselves than with the people or missions they serve. Politicians, executives, celebrities, and those who are simply famous for being famous dominate our current cultural landscape.

Social media has only magnified this trend. It's created an entire industry around the concept of the "influencer," where individuals can make fortunes by broadcasting every detail of their daily lives. The underlying assumption is that these people are important enough for the world to care about what they're doing, thinking, eating, watching, or how they're working out, every hour of the day.

The age of narcissism is not just emerging—it's well established. I've lost count of how many athletes, celebrities, or public figures, when honored or drafted into their professional leagues, begin their speech with something like, "First of all, I'd like to thank myself."

But an ego out of control always leads to destruction. So, as leaders, how do we recognize when narcissism is creeping in? How do we know if we're slipping into patterns that put self at the center? How do we keep our ego in its proper place?

It's often easy to see the wake left by someone's ego—the chaos, the confusion, the exhaustion they leave behind. It's harder to recognize the wake we are creating. Yet we all leave one. And when we lose sight of humility, when ego takes the lead, our wake can be equally exhausting for those who follow us.

It's worth pausing here for a moment of self-reflection. Have you ever found yourself thinking thoughts like:

> *I think I'm pretty great, and you should too.*
> *I don't need to apologize—just trust me and move on.*
> *This place would fall apart without me.*
> *I hope they appreciate all I've done around here.*
> *I can criticize you freely, but don't you dare come for me.*

When thoughts like these surface, we're flirting with the kind of destruction that unchecked ego inevitably brings.

Cultivating Humility

So, how do we lead with a healthy sense of self, grounded in humility, so that the wake we leave behind is smooth and life-giving rather than rough and depleting?

The ancient book of Proverbs suggests that *wisdom* is the key. Throughout Scripture—and history—we see a consistent truth: *No wise man is ever arrogant.* In fact, arrogance is the giveaway, the telltale symptom of ignorance. Proverbs links humility and pride to nearly every good or bad outcome. While wisdom is crucial for making sound decisions, it's humility that makes our relationships with God, with others, and even with ourselves healthy and sustainable.

Growing up, I (Matt) can remember a number of lessons taught to me by a variety of family members and mentors that generally suggested humility "was not thinking less of yourself, but thinking of yourself less." If that is true, and I believe it is, this means both "I'm the best" and "I'm the worst" are prideful statements because both are self-focused. True humility refuses to keep the spotlight on the self, whether in praise or in self-pity. At its core, humility is wisdom's assessment of self. It's not self-loathing, timidity, or insecurity. It's not a low view of self—it's a *right* or *healthy* view of self.

Humility is hard to define, but it's unmistakable when you see it—and just as clear when you don't. Humble leaders don't manage their image or push themselves to the front. They honor others by valuing their needs as equal to their own.

Of course, it's natural to want to be seen, appreciated, and valued. But humility doesn't mean denying that desire or thinking poorly of ourselves. It flows from honest self-awareness—from knowing who we are and, even more importantly, *whose* we are. Over and over in Scripture, we see warnings against pride:

> "When pride comes, then comes disgrace, but with humility comes wisdom" (Proverbs 11:2).
>
> "God opposes the proud but shows favor to the humble" (James 4:6).
>
> "Pride goes before destruction, and a haughty spirit before a fall" (Proverbs 16:18).

Leader, pride will destroy you. And an ego out of control will always lead to destruction.

The Best–and Humblest–of Leaders

By every measure, Jesus Christ was the greatest leader to ever walk this earth—from his level of influence to his follower count to the impact he has made across time. Whether you're a Christian or not, Jesus' ability to lead people was, and remains, undeniable.

Balancing our pride and keeping our ego in check is a key component of living and leading like Jesus. Humility is one of the highest attributes Jesus modeled for his followers, as we see in Philippians 2:3–11:

> Do nothing out of selfish ambition or vain conceit. Rather, in humility value others above yourselves, not looking to your own interests but each of you to the interests of the others. In your relationships with one another, have the same mindset as Christ Jesus: Who, being in very nature God, did not consider equality with God something to be used to his own advantage; rather, he made himself nothing by taking the very nature of a servant, being made in human likeness. And being found in appearance as a man, he humbled himself by becoming obedient to death—even death on a cross! Therefore God exalted him to the highest place and gave him the name that is above every name, that at the name of Jesus every knee should bow, in heaven and on earth and under the earth, and every tongue acknowledge that Jesus Christ is Lord, to the glory of God the Father.

No one will ever be greater than Jesus. And no one will ever be more humble than Jesus. Greatness and humility go hand in hand. Jesus humbly allowed himself to die on that cruel cross for each of us, knowing in our pride we would often think too highly of ourselves. Jesus should serve as our model for all we do, even the amount of humility we exhibit in our own leadership journeys.

As Jesus' followers, we are commanded to imitate his example of humble sacrifice. One of the details of Dr. Jackson's character I love is the fact that he always parked in the back of the lot. He didn't consider himself so high and mighty that he deserved the best parking spot. In this small way, he imitated Christ's sacrificial humility.

I (Matt) often think of the image of a boat racing through the water and the wake it leaves. As leaders, we all leave a wake. Those who seek to lead from the Core will choose to lead and live in such a way as to minimize the chaos and complexity for those who are following. A person infused with this sort of humility is at ease in their own skin. They are free from the pressure to self-promote or prove their worth. Their identity doesn't come from accolades or accomplishments but from the One who knows and loves them completely. May we all develop and demonstrate this type of self-awareness and keep our egos in check.

Embrace Truth

I (Matt), like most people, love a good story. I've been exposed to thousands of them in my life, yet when faced with a choice to listen to facts and data or an interesting story, I'll choose a story every time. I love stories so much that I wrote my doctoral dissertation about a leader's strategic use of storytelling to navigate organizational change.

A good story contains a captivating plot, engaging characters, and a hero and a villain. Good stories can provide a comedic moment of relief or a suspenseful moment that allows you to feel the pain of the characters. Most stories also contain a climactic scene that brings everything together and provides a lesson. Each of these core elements is critical to unleashing the power of a story.

Leaders listen to stories all day long. In some ways, it's our entire job description. Things get tricky, though, when we are tasked with hearing multiple stories about the same situation. As Proverbs 18:17

says, "In a lawsuit the first to speak seems right, until someone comes forward and cross-examines." If the leader listens to only one story, makes a decision, and then acts on that decision, it could be a wrong decision because it might not be based on truth. The best kind of leader takes in multiple points of view and considers the truth in each one.

This leads us to Core leadership principle number three: *Embrace the truth.* Our ability to absorb, understand, and make sense of the stories taking place around us in our organizations, families, churches, and communities is directly tied to our ability to lead.

Embracing truth involves two key components. The first is searching for and finding the truth. The second is accepting and acting on it. One of the most well-known sayings of Jesus is: "Therefore everyone who hears these words of mine and puts them into practice is like a wise man who built his house on the rock" (Matthew 7:24). He compares the wise man to someone who built his house on a rock. Great forces of wind and rain come against the house, but it remains solid. In like manner, the wise leader hears words of truth and puts them into practice. Thus, the wise leader builds from a core that cannot be easily shaken.

Embracing the truth is an easy principle to comprehend, but it can be difficult to put into practice. All of us struggle with embracing the truth, and some never learn how to do it. But make no mistake—how a leader accepts and chooses to deal with truth is directly correlated to that leader's success.

Over the years of leading organizations and coaching leaders, we've found it helpful to distinguish between two layers of truth. We'll call them level-one truth and level-two truth.

Level-One Truth

Level-one truth is the kind of truth every leader must have. Each day of organizational life begs for the truth to be known before operational decisions can be accurately made.

Level-one truth is the easiest type of truth to deal with. We all rely on facts and data to establish truth. We saw this come to light in the story of Dr. Jackson when he discovered accounting errors revealing a potential scam with a large vendor. Leaders must be careful, willing, and eager to hear all the facts or to see all the data, knowing that without it, a wrong decision can easily be made.

There's one element of a story I haven't yet mentioned: the *context*. The information around a story can make or break the entire saga. Imagine for a moment that *The Lord of the Rings* was set not in the vast mountain ranges of New Zealand but in New York City. It would change everything, wouldn't it?

Leaders must be aware of the context in which their organizations and teams exist. Consistent contextual analyses provide the truths we need to not only work for the good of the people but to move our organizations forward. Leaders rely on resources like consultants and SWOT analyses to better understand the impact of external factors like competition, legal and regulatory environments, and societal and cultural changes. They're also aware of internal factors, such as resource and personnel challenges, culture and office politics, and team dynamics. All of these factors impact the setting, or context, of the organizational story.

Our stories are dynamic, existing in a changing world. "The way it's always been done" seldom meets the new demands of reality in a change-oriented environment. The only way to keep up is to analyze the data and see the trends. One must be able to spot those areas in which an organization is no longer performing well. One must watch the competition. Thus, the eyes of the leader are always looking. The ears are always listening. Our great quest is to answer the question "What is the truth?" Without it, good decisions are impossible.

Level-one truth becomes paramount in major acquisitions. When one company buys another, perhaps two CEOs or two boards agree in principle, but that's only the beginning. Lawyers, accountants, and other pertinent entities begin to search for the facts, trying to determine if everything is as it appears on the surface. Or they begin looking at data to establish true values. The truth allows both the buyer and the seller to be treated fairly, allowing the deal to come to fruition—unless some discovery is made that results in one party backing out.

The truth does not always reveal pretty facts, and leaders must embrace this reality. No leader gets very far without encountering issues with employees. At times, employees must be corrected, disciplined, put on probation, or terminated. Every case is unique and requires thoughtful examination of the story. There are often multiple sides to these types of stories presented, each of which may be neither true nor false. It's only a set of words spoken from a particular perspective. Weighing the available data and listening to differing viewpoints is critical to making the right call.

Level-Two Truth

Level-two truth moves beyond the organizational to the personal. As you might suspect, personal truth is often more difficult to accept, navigate, and ultimately embrace. It's possible, and very common, for one to become an expert at seeking and finding truth at the organizational level while being a significant failure at the personal level. It can be much easier to see the problems around us than to see the problems within us.

If you are practicing the first two Core principles—working for the good of the people and keeping your ego in check—you will be predisposed to look for and act upon personal truths. You will seek out honest feedback from people you trust—those who want to see you succeed. You will allow your team to describe your "wake" and make appropriate adjustments.

Searching for level two-truth requires the ability to be introspective. Level-two truth questions can sound like this:

- What causes me to be short-tempered?
- What is underlying my persistent negativism?
- What has happened to my passion for this work?
- What habits are limiting me from becoming a more effective leader?
- What is important to me at this point in my life?
- What is causing distance between my spouse and me?

The truth is not just about what's going on around us. It's also about what's going on inside of us. While each of us is wonderfully made with many positive qualities, we all have insecurities and flaws. Each and every leader also has blind spots they may or may not fully recognize in their own life. A leader's job is to "move the needle" for themselves and their organization every day. But how can one move the needle if they don't even realize that the needle needs to be moved? That's why leaders need to search for level-two truth.

A list of potential ways a leader can have truth revealed to them may include the objective perspectives provided by counseling, spiritual direction, and executive or leadership coaching. Personality or productivity assessments can open our eyes to truths about how we are wired and what makes us unique. Often these types of opportunities are provided by the leader's organization. Leaders who embrace truth create organizations that are better prepared to handle the realities in front of them with clarity, good decision-making, and confidence.

The Courage to Embrace Truth

By this point in our study of the leadership Core, it should be obvious that good leadership is rare. Why is this the case? Well, how many truly unselfish leaders do you know who are working for the good of others and speaking up for their welfare? And how many of those people are working to keep their ego in check? How many of them are serious truth seekers? And, if they're good at seeking truth at level one, how many of them are willing to leap into level two?

No wonder leadership is so difficult! It takes courage for someone to willingly search for the truth and act upon it.

Unfortunately, we've seen countless examples of moments when leaders are confronted with the truth, and yet they choose to take everyone for a ride in the "spin zone" so they can tell their side of the story. The trends say the business is going in the wrong direction, but the leader doesn't act. The data says one area of the company is unprofitable, but the leader does nothing. A discovery is made that a key employee has a personal problem that is hindering company performance, but the leader ignores it or gets defensive about it. These are all level-one truth issues. And when you're dealing with these types of situations, it's difficult to imagine venturing to level two.

Let's take it a step further. Of all those in leadership who accept and act on level-one truth, how many can and do go a step further into the level-two world? Level two is personal: *What is the truth about me, and what must I do about it?* It's embracing the hardest kind of truth, and few are willing to dive into this deep and often self-imposed forbidden world.

I (Matt) knew of an organization whose CEO spent their entire tenure putting a positive spin on a problematic internal situation. For a while, the team and board of directors bought into the narrative. But about two-thirds of the way through their tenure, reality caught up. Word reached the CEO that "the honeymoon was over"—employees and other key stakeholders were no longer buying the spin. The core KPIs, data analytics, and overall results simply didn't align with the story the CEO was telling. Organizational morale hit a new low. Yet the CEO continued broadcasting their version of reality to anyone who would listen. It didn't help—and things continued to unravel.

Consultants were brought in to assess key aspects of the organization and, ultimately, to deliver a clear-eyed report to the CEO. As part of their process, the consultants met with senior executives beforehand to share their findings and gather input on how best to deliver the message. The executives encouraged them to be direct, knowing the CEO would likely resist anything that challenged their narrative.

More than once, those consultants walked out of their meetings with the CEO feeling demoralized, ridiculed, and berated for supposedly not understanding what was "really" going on. These were professionals who had worked with successful organizations across the country, yet they were stunned at how their data-driven insights had been twisted to present a completely different version of reality.

In fact, on more than one occasion, the consultants ended up sending final reports to the executive team that were drastically watered down from what they'd originally intended to present. When asked why, they eventually confided that there were two main reasons.

First, they had grown to respect the executive team and feared how a "truthful" report might hurt them or their work under such a resistant leader.

Second, they knew that any recommendations differing from the CEO's narrative would be dismissed. Worse, the CEO would retaliate by publicly discrediting them and their firm. The consultants essentially decided to preserve their reputation, exit the engagement as quietly as possible, and return once a new CEO was in place.

Now, you and I can debate whether the consultants made the right call. But don't miss the point: This CEO's inability to embrace the truth created a wake so toxic that even seasoned consultants—those used to navigating tough organizational dynamics—were willing to risk their credibility to protect the team more than the leader ever did.

Most consultants aim to finish the job well and earn future business. But in this case, they wanted nothing more to do with the CEO, and the organization suffered even more as a result of one leader's unwillingness to face reality.

Embracing Truth

Our Core leadership principles build on each other and are interconnected. Leaders are humble people who, at their deepest level, are committed to working for those who follow them. They are relentless seekers of truth, and when truth is found, they are courageous enough to act upon it. To make progress, whether organizational or personal, leaders must start with the truth.

Before we move to the next Core principle, pause and ask yourself the following questions:

- How well do I accept the truth?
- Am I willing to embrace the truth? Or do I push back when the truth is presented?
- Do I have people on my team who are able to tell me the truth, no matter how hard it is to hear? If I'm surrounded by "yes men and women," what could I do to change this dynamic? Who could I appoint as the official "truth teller"?
- Does our organization have a culture of truth telling? If not, how could I model and invite this habit into our midst?

Wise leaders embrace the truth and act upon it. Once you summon the courage to seek and find the truth, it will become a precious gift for you—one you can use for the good of your organization and all the people in it.

Chapter 18

Lead with Your Ears

I (Matt) am originally from West Texas, where there is little to no rain and the wind blows regularly, yet somehow agriculture is the basis for the region's economy. Out there, the weather is one of the most commonly discussed topics, aside from football, the price of gas, and how our country isn't quite what it used to be. Growing up, there was little to no use for ideas that came out of the "big cities." Ideas that originated from "up North," "back East," or the "West Coast" were often found to be suspicious and not always tolerated.

For Thanksgiving, we often traveled to visit family just outside San Antonio. I remember one year—I think I was in ninth grade—when, as we gathered around the dinner table, the conversation turned to the oddest craze of 1994. We assumed it was a new trend, yet apparently it was an old idea that had been repackaged for a new generation.

Some of my family members had discovered earwax candles, and they were hooked. Not only that, but they were convinced the entire family should try them.

Now, a quick word about earwax candles for those who may have missed this cultural phenomenon. There was a time in our nation's history when it was considered both safe and beneficial to one's health to stick a special candle in your ear and light it on fire. The theory was that the heat would draw out the earwax, improving not just hearing but overall wellness because, at the time, overall health was linked to the health of one's ears. I know it sounds . . . well, interesting. But it *was* a thing, I promise.

As a fourteen-year-old West Texan, I thought this was the craziest idea I'd ever heard. I was sure my family would denounce such foolishness. Soon, the conversation shifted to more familiar topics—probably the weather, gas prices, or the upcoming Dallas Cowboys game—and I moved on, forgetting all about ear candles.

That is, until the next day.

I walked into my aunt and uncle's house and witnessed one of the most unbelievable scenes my innocent teenage eyes had ever seen. Gathered around the kitchen counter were many of my family members—the same ones who'd raised me to be skeptical of anything out of the ordinary. I saw my grandfather (maybe the wisest person I've ever known), my parents, aunts, and even an uncle—each with a burning candle sticking out of their ear.

Another uncle stood by with scissors, apparently assigned to trim the candles as they burned so the wax wouldn't drip or start a fire.

I couldn't believe what I was seeing.

After the "treatment," several of them claimed they could hear better. It was a miracle! Well, maybe not a miracle—but it definitely made an impression.

Maybe it really *was* all about the ears.

And yes, I know what you're wondering: Did I try it? I did. But I can't say I noticed a difference. I think I was mostly in awe that my family was enthusiastically embracing something so outside the norm.

The earwax-candle craze seemed to fade away, but from time to time, it does come up in our family stories. Almost a decade later, I took my then-girlfriend to this same house for Thanksgiving with the same people, and you know what they did? They put a candle in her ear and set it on fire. I suppose it served as some rite of passage into the family, because I proposed two days later and she said yes.

The image of smart, wise, cautious people experimenting with ear candles will never go away for me. Nor has the principle for life and leadership that comes when one is carefully paying attention to their ears. The idea of so much significance being placed on the importance of the ears for overall health connects to leadership as well. I would suggest that "healthy" leadership has a great deal to do with how well we utilize our ears and truly listen.

Lead with Your Ears

I suspect that, like me, you've heard many lessons on the importance of truly listening to others. One of the most cited passages in Scripture on this topic is James 1:19: "Everyone should be quick to listen, slow to speak and slow to become angry." I've always appreciated the traditional wording of that verse, but one day, while reading Eugene Peterson's modern translation, *The Message*, it hit me in a new way and became a core principle in my life: "Post this at all the intersections, dear friends: Lead with your ears, follow up with your tongue, and let anger struggle along in the rear."

Did you catch that? *Lead with your ears.*

James urges a response that begins with listening. As leaders, we must resist the "plugged-ear foolishness" that can so easily take hold. If we want to lead others well—especially for their good—we must recognize that one of the first things God needs to clear out of our lives is whatever's blocking our ability to hear.

The kind of foolishness described throughout Proverbs is difficult to root out, partly because it's hard to recognize, especially in ourselves. And if our ears are closed off, we may never even realize it's there. But before we can be known for godly character and wise counsel, our ears need to be open.

If you've spent any time around children, you've probably seen what some kids do when they don't want to hear something: They put their hands over ears, make loud noises, or totally shut down. As adults—and as leaders—we often do our own version of the same thing. We've just developed more sophisticated ways of not listening.

Don't believe me?

Maybe a friend invited you to lunch to gently confront you about how you've been treating others. You might have responded with "Thanks for bringing this to my attention" or "I appreciate your input." But then, as soon as you got back in your car, you vowed never to meet with that person again—and later told someone else, "Can you believe what they said to me?"

That's not listening. That's polite deflection.

Leading with our ears begins in our personal lives, but it also extends into our professional world. Imagine you've hired a consultant to assess an underperforming part of your organization. You've been deeply involved with this team for six months, sharing all your best ideas and tasking them with building a plan based entirely on your approach. They tried to offer their perspective, but you were convinced you already knew what was needed. So, your team carried out your vision—despite lacking confidence in it—and sidelined the strategies they believed could actually help.

When the consultant arrives, not only are the numbers still slipping, but team morale has taken a hit. A few days later, the consultant presents her findings, only to have you dismiss her insights and blame your team for poor execution. You decide to hold another meeting to "clarify" your ideas, certain the issue is that they just didn't understand your vision.

Moments like this reveal plugged ears and alive-and-well foolishness.

Many times in my life, God has used wise people to speak truth I didn't want to hear. Sometimes I listened, sometimes I didn't. But my prayer for you as a leader is this: When truth finds you, listen—and *really* hear it.

My wife, Kagney (yes, the same woman who survived the earwax candle incident), would be the first to tell you I'm still a work in progress when it comes to this. Despite my best efforts to lead with my ears, I still fall short.

Being a good listener is hard. It takes practice and patience. In *Life Together*, Dietrich Bonhoeffer warned against "a kind of listening with half an ear that presumes already to know what the other person has to say." He called it "an impatient, inattentive listening . . . only waiting for a chance to speak."

As driven and busy leaders, we often assume we know where a conversation is going and start crafting a reply before the speaker even finishes. Or we're caught in the middle of something we think is more important, distracted by yet another meeting or looming deadline, and we stop listening, silently wishing the person talking would just wrap it up. Or—let's be honest—we simply allow ourselves to be half-eared, our attention divided by the constant pull of competing priorities.

Proverbs 29:20 says: "Observe the people who always talk before they think—even simpletons are better off than they are" (MSG). If we believe that leadership is for the good of the people, we must never forget that poor listening diminishes others. Intentional, focused listening, on the other hand, affirms their value. It shows them they matter.

Becoming a Listener Who Leads

To lead with our ears the way Dr. Jackson modeled for us, we must be fully engaged with both ears and committed to truly hearing what others are saying. This means silencing the noise around us. It may require us to delay the next meeting, turn off our phone notifications, and show up with stillness, relaxed body language, and an open, welcoming posture.

It takes energy to block out distractions and prioritize the person in front of us. Listening isn't a one-time task—it's a continual act.

We're not just called to be quick to listen but to *keep listening*. Only when we do this can we grasp the fuller picture of truth we're meant to consider and embrace.

Leading with our ears also means cultivating the habit of asking good questions. The book of Proverbs repeatedly affirms this approach. It is the fool, Proverbs 18:2 tells us, who "takes no pleasure in understanding, but only in expressing his opinion" (ESV). And verse 13 adds: "If one gives an answer before he hears, it is his folly and shame" (ESV). Listening requires curiosity. It means diving below the surface to understand the interior world of others. As Proverbs 20:5 says, "The purposes of a person's heart are deep waters, but one who has insight draws them out."

This is the heart of leadership Core coaching. The best coaches specialize in asking thoughtful, open-ended questions—designed not to interrogate but to invite reflection. They listen for verbal and nonverbal cues and create an environment where people feel safe going deeper. Through careful, intentional questions, they guide others toward new ways of thinking.

Leading with your ears isn't just good coaching—it's also vital for effective service to others. In *Life Together*, Dietrich Bonhoeffer once said that "listening can be a greater service than speaking." Many of our most important leadership moments won't take place in front of a crowd or in a big meeting. They'll happen across a table, leaning in and making eye contact, giving someone the space to be seen and heard.

Leaders who commit to listening must also resist the impulse to fix every problem. Often people don't need solutions right away—they simply need space to express their emotions. Sometimes just being able to share what's on their heart diffuses the tension and helps bring clarity.

Psychologists and counselors often say that good listening is less about finding the perfect response and more about affirming the person who's speaking. Also in *Life Together*, Bonhoeffer put it this way: "Often a person can be helped merely by having someone who will listen to him seriously."

In my work with leaders across different sectors, I've noticed a common concern: Even those who are committed to people-first leadership often feel uncertain about what to say or when to speak up.

I remember this type of situation happening early in my career. The university had hired me to work in the university's fundraising department. I was young and inexperienced, especially for a major gifts officer. To help me learn, my new boss brought in a seasoned fundraising consultant to spend a few hours with me. I admitted I was nervous about asking people for money, and even more nervous about not knowing what to say if they asked tough questions.

That afternoon, I learned one lesson that stuck with me and has served me well not just in fundraising but throughout my leadership journey. The consultant told me, "Listen for gifts." He explained that the less I talked and the more I listened, the more I would begin to hear what truly moved people—their passions, their interests, and their values. I would be able to understand what kind of impact they wanted to make and even how much they might be willing to give.

"If you listen closely enough," the consultant said, "the answers to your questions will show up." He was right. Real listening doesn't just give us answers—it helps us discern what to say and when to say it. Listening lies at the core of leadership because it gives us access to the hearts of those around us.

Listening Is Not an Ear Issue, It's a Heart Issue

The ancient book of Proverbs says a lot about hearing, but it's not talking about our ears—whether we have good hearing or a diagnosed issue. That's because listening is a heart issue, not an ear issue. Listening is a choice. We can choose to truly hear and respond to what's being said, or we can fall into the trap of selective hearing—listening without really getting what the other person is saying.

As you reflect on your own leadership skills and the principle of leading with your ears, consider this: On a scale of 1 to 10 (with 10 being the highest), how would you rate your ability to listen to your employees, family members, or team members? And how would they rate you?

While reading this, maybe a moment, a season, or a specific role has come to mind—one where you didn't lead with your ears. Maybe you didn't like the data being shared, or you disagreed with the perspective of the person sharing it. How could you have responded differently?

Recently I found myself walking through a local pharmacy that had a small section of alternative or more "natural" approaches to health. I grinned when I saw up, in the corner of a display case, a package of earwax candles. I remembered that moment all those years ago when my family, at least for that season, became obsessed with the health benefits of taking care of one's ears. All these years later, I believe the connection to the ears and a person's leadership health is more than just the latest fad. It is a core principle to remember. For many, listening or leading with the ears is a real challenge. To those who may struggle with this principle. I encourage you to take heart—you're not alone in this. But don't brush it off either. Those who are serious about leading for the good of others must make listening a core part of who they are.

CHAPTER 19

Show Up with Grace

In my work as a leadership consultant, I (Matt) came across a scenario in a mid-sized company where a new leader had recently stepped up as CEO, and hopes were high. She was sharp, articulate, and confident, and truly seemed to know her stuff.

In her early days, the CEO was frequently invited to speak—internally and externally—about her favorite topic: leadership. She championed emotional intelligence, constructive feedback, and self-awareness, encouraging everyone to examine their blind spots. Her presentations were polished, her quotes memorable, and her presence compelling.

But as the months passed, financial pressures began to mount. Revenue lagged behind the company's needs. Those who had hoped for a miracle worker realized that even the new CEO's skills couldn't reverse the challenges overnight. And as the pressure increased, cracks began to form in the fabric of the organization.

Despite her emphasis on trust and empowerment, the new CEO's leadership style shifted toward control. Meetings became rigid. Growth goals turned unrealistic. Though she continued to speak publicly about the importance of "our people," internally, it became clear that people were no longer the priority.

She tried to manage everything herself—every decision, every plan—leaving little room for collaboration. Over time, morale and retention plummeted. And the hope that had once surrounded her leadership faded away.

Ironically, even as she lost touch with her team, she continued delivering talks on emotional intelligence and self-awareness, oblivious to the growing disconnect between her words and actions. The more difficult things became, the harder she pushed her message. The CEO didn't realize she was losing the people. And by the time it became clear to her what was happening, it was already too late.

Show Up with Grace

This story is all too familiar. When pressure mounts, our leadership presence is tested, which is where Core leadership principle number five comes into play: *Show up with grace.*

The word *grace* has a lot of meaning packed into it, but for the purpose of this book, we will define it as "the way a leader acts." It's being controlled, polite, caring, kind, thoughtful, compassionate, and generous. Leaders who work for the good of their people and lead from the Core show up with grace, maintaining a steadfast presence under pressure.

Leading from the Core is less about telling people how to conduct themselves or prescribing how they get their work done and more about showing up for them every day. We're talking about literally, physically showing up—like Dr. Jackson going out of his way to attend the funeral of his employee's husband.

Emotional intelligence (also known as EQ)—not intellect—is often the key to a leader's success. In EQ workshops, participants are asked to recall a leader they deeply respected and list the qualities that earned their esteem. As responses are shared, a clear pattern emerges: Rarely do people highlight intelligence or technical skill. Instead, they name traits like *humility, honesty, kindness, courage,* and *generosity.* The takeaway? Followers value leaders not for what they know but for how they behave. A leader's credibility is built on consistent character and presence, especially under pressure, not on their IQ or business acumen. *How* a leader shows up is what matters most.

Consistently showing up with grace allows leaders to speak truth to their team. Truth is hard to find, hear, and accept—and even harder to speak. Yet leaders must not only uncover truth but communicate it, especially when it requires change. If an organization must shift, or an individual must grow, the truth must be shared. But how it's delivered matters deeply. When leaders speak with fear, anger, or harshness, the message often fails. Scolding or cold delivery—even when the truth is necessary—produces resistance.

Think of a time someone shared a hard truth with you. Was it a spouse, a child, or a supervisor? How they said it likely shaped your response. In their book *Boundaries,* Dr. Henry Cloud and Dr. John Townsend note that if truth comes harshly—loud, demeaning, or unkind—it's often rejected. But truth spoken with compassion and care is more likely to be embraced. They wrote, "Truth without love is always seen as judgment. When we speak truth, it must be seasoned with grace. People rarely respond well to harsh truth, but truth spoken in love can heal and restore."

Even when truth carries difficult consequences, wise leaders deliver it with grace, because people matter more than the hard truths they must face. Leaders should generously offer grace because the time will come when they need it in return. We are all going to make a mess of things from time to time. Everyone has the potential to completely botch the big deal or make a wrong decision that negatively impacts the rest of the organization. When that happens, we will hope to receive grace. And often grace is shown to leaders in organizations when they have shown it themselves.

A few years ago, a well-established leader made a massive mistake. It became a public relations nightmare for their organization. The leader, whose entire tenure had been defined internally by bullying people and being notoriously transactional with team members, could not understand why very few people were willing to come to his defense when his mistake became public. But many in the organization felt he was getting what he deserved. Why should they show him grace when he had never shown it to them?

People in that organization developed a mantra for themselves and others to live by: *Where there is no relationship, there is no grace.*

How we show up for others in our leadership creates the platform on which we stand as we seek to be influential. So, how do you show up in all situations—when you are angry, when you need to lead your team through a crisis, when times are wonderful, when days are ordinary, when you don't feel well? People are always watching, and they are particularly observant of your presence. Those who follow will take their lead in any given situation more from how you react and the moves you make than they will from the words you say.

What's Your Leadership Brand?

Today, we hear a lot about "personal brands," not just in marketing but in everyday leadership. In the age of influencers and brand ambassadors, many strive to build a brand that earns recognition and influence. Marketing experts often discuss the basics of what makes a brand strong. Many will point to the consistency of the interactions that customers have with a company as a significant factor in brand strength. Other items related to the strength of an organization's brand include its continued relevance even in changing seasons or times. Other marketing professionals would suggest that an organization's distinctiveness, or its ability to stand out when compared to other similar companies, also creates a strong brand.

While the core elements of a strong brand—consistency, relevance, and distinctiveness—remain the same, I was once challenged to think about my leadership brand in a more meaningful way, and the insight still resonates.

Leaders often work hard to shape the narrative of their leadership—especially when thinking about legacy. They want to define how others will remember them, crafting stories that highlight vision, strategy, and impact. But they fail to miss a key truth: *Your leadership brand is the stories others tell about you, not the ones you tell about yourself.*

Your brand lives in the memories and experiences of the people you've led. Like the employees who spoke at Dr. Jackson's retirement party, one day people will have something to say about you. Your brand is revealed in how people felt under your leadership—day by day, moment by moment. That can be a sobering reality.

In a world obsessed with image, here's an idea that cuts through the noise: Leadership is not about how you *present* yourself but how you *impact* others. And the stories others tell about you will last far longer than any you attempt to script yourself.

We create our brand by the way we consistently show up for those in our care. Do people's experiences with you remain consistent when things are going well and when they are not? Are you all over the place or are you steady and stable? Do you get overly excited when something happens or are you the one in the room who doesn't flinch? Are you moody and people worry about which version of you they will interact with on a daily basis? These questions and so many more like them are what help us to understand more fully our personal brand. So one more question for you is this:

What leadership brand are you building?

The Five Elements of a Graceful Leadership Presence

Your leadership presence—how you show up for your people—matters just as much as any strategy or technique you employ. Your presence can either build trust or destroy it. Your presence can either instill confidence or impart anxiety. Your presence can either invite people to engage or push them away. Quite frankly, your leadership presence determines whether or not others will choose to follow you.

There are five essential elements to a grace-filled leadership presence: character, self-awareness, self-control, courage, and awareness for life.

Element #1: Character

Character is the foundation upon which leaders build a successful life—inside and outside of your organization. And nothing destroys success more than a lack of character.

Scanning the literature of leadership, it's clear to see book after book, study after study, story after story detail leadership failures. These derailments are seldom due to a lack of technical skill or personal ability. Rather, they stem from a failure of personal character. There is no substitute for character. Good character allows talents and abilities to hit their intended mark. Lack of it always results in failure.

Character is the internal fabric of your being, revealing the condition of your heart. Jesus once said that out of the heart come all the issues of life. Truth or lies, integrity or dishonesty, good or evil, humility or pride, purity or impurity, optimism or pessimism—all have their launching pad in the heart. Surely that is the reason we are called upon so often to examine our hearts.

Character is a prerequisite for taking advice and correction. In his book *Necessary Endings*, Dr. Henry Cloud describes three types of people: wise, foolish, and evil. He defines wise people as those who are open to hearing hard truths about themselves, even when they'd rather ignore them. They know their imperfections and limited abilities, and they welcome words that provide correction.

The great news about character is that it can change. No one needs to stay stuck in lies, evil, impurity, or dishonesty. Though change will never be easy, it *can* be done. It all starts with desire. You must *want* to improve your character, which takes discipline and hard work.

The late teacher Jim Rohn taught me (Ken) years ago that you need to work harder on yourself than you work on any other single thing. Many leaders who experience failure or derailment are hard workers—they're just working on the wrong things.

Life's difficulties can either build or destroy character, and the difference is up to you. Health challenges, relationship struggles, the death of loved ones, financial problems, fear and anxiety, and a host of other elements can produce major storms in our lives. In each storm we face, we can choose to be either a victim or a student. Choosing to be a student in a storm of life will always change us for the better. It will always speed our growth in character.

Those who lead from the Core know they must work on their own hearts and be people of unquestioned character so they will be ready to have the inner strength to stand up when the storms of life inevitably appear.

Two: Self-Awareness

Leadership presence is inseparably linked to self-awareness, which is knowing yourself and how your mood and behavior impact others.

Do you understand what causes you anxiety? Do you know what makes you feel competent and comfortable? Do you have a good idea of where you are naturally gifted? Hopefully, the answer is yes, which is the first step in the process of self-awareness.

Leadership presence is about knowing yourself and regulating how you act according to that knowledge. Have you ever found yourself sitting in a meeting with your colleagues, and a decision is made about a topic or agenda item that you disagree with passionately? If so, how did you act? Did you raise your voice, stomp your fist on the table, leave without saying anything? Or did you take a deep breath, re-state your thoughts on the subject in a different way, keep your calm, or ask a new question to better understand the decision? Disagreements happen all the time, and I am not calling for leaders to be pushovers. I am suggesting that leaders need to consider the bigger picture, play the long game, and regulate their responses so as not to create a more significant problem.

Developing self-awareness in isolation is like trying to shave or put on makeup without a mirror. All of us need some level of feedback to understand how we come across. To lead from the Core, you must develop some sort of reflection practice, whether through journaling, counseling, or prayer. You must also invite others to share open and honest feedback with you, which goes back to our principle of seeking out the truth and acting upon it. You must learn not to take yourself too seriously.

To begin this process of reflection, answer the following questions, paying attention to how you feel about your responses:

- How do I react when a direct report or significant team member in my organization tells me they're leaving for a new opportunity?

- What words would other people use to describe my typical mood?
- When I enter a room, how do people respond?

In order to have a strong leadership presence, one must come to grips with who they are from the inside out and be honest about how that makes a difference in the lives they lead.

Three: Self-Control

Nowhere is leadership presence more important than in intense emotional settings. We once consulted with a young leader who worked closely with the CEO of his organization. Outside the CEO's office was a group of couches where the next individual or group would wait for their turn to enter. Like many CEOs, this individual had a strong personality. He was often stressed out and prone to anger.

It became somewhat of a ritual for the group leaving the CEO's office to give an update regarding the CEO's mood to the group sitting on the couches. If the CEO was having "one of those days," the waiting group would receive a certain look, a hushed update, or a friendly warning. Each person entering the office knew part of their role was to prepare the next person for what was to come. Essentially, the members of the organization created signals to help each other deal with the "leader" so that fewer people would have to endure the pain of having a negative interaction with the boss.

It should not be this way. This is not how leaders act. This is how immature children act. Self-control is the ability to rein yourself in, not permitting your emotions to carry you—and your organization—away.

People can become easily frightened and prone to panic. In their fear, they tend to get angry. They say ugly things. They make untrue accusations. It's human nature. And leaders deal with it all the time. Thus, leadership presence is often defined—and sometimes permanently defined—by the reaction of the leader to the exaggerated reactions of others.

One of the greatest stories of leadership comes from the book of Exodus in the Bible, when Moses led the Israelites across the Red Sea. They had just escaped slavery in the most powerful empire on earth, Egypt. Pharaoh had been subjected to humiliation and defeat, finally allowing the Israelites to leave his land and his control.

But as soon as the Israelites were gone, Pharaoh changed his mind and sent his army after them, with every intention to kill and destroy. The Egyptians caught up to the Israelites at the edge of the Red Sea, and the escaping people were alarmed. There was no place to run—they were completely hemmed in by the sea. With no ability to fight, they were totally helpless and terrified. And so they did what people tend to do in those situations: They panicked and blamed their leader for getting them into this situation.

Please don't miss the point: Leaders are *always* the brunt of blame and criticism when followers become afraid, uncertain, and uncomfortable.

In this story, Moses was a classic example of great leadership presence. He stood before the people and told them to be calm. He assured them they would be okay.

As I write this, it's been a week since a terrorist attack in California where fourteen people lost their lives. Just this morning, news agencies are telling the story of one of the police officers involved in the rescue of those who were saved in the attack. Of course, the people being attacked were terrified and in a state of extreme fear and panic. This officer stood among them and said, "It will be okay. I will take a bullet before I let a bullet get to you."

That, my friends, is leadership presence. And that is exactly what Moses did. He stood before the people and assured them it would be okay.

Upon close reading of this story, it becomes obvious that even as Moses was assuring the people, he, too, was full of anxiety. He, too, was wondering what would happen next. But even with that being true, he was able to maintain a non-anxious presence before those people whose fear had driven away all ability to reason.

Self-control is the ability to maintain graceful presence under pressure. There is an "old-school" word that I often use when working with leaders, especially as it relates to one's ability to control themselves in stressful situations. The word is *savvy*. There are a number of ways to define what savvy is, but generally speaking, the way I like to use it has to do with one's ability to be perceptive and understand how to resist impulses strategically and wisely. Another way to think about how savvy connects to self-control has to do with the ability to read the room and assess a situation and its potential consequences with a sense of control that generates trust and respect. A person who possesses self-control and operates with savvy is able to resist impulses and lead strategically and wisely in directions that align with their organization's long-term goals.

Sometimes even the leaders who exhibit the greatest levels of self-control find themselves in situations that seem dire, and when fear closes in, people look to their leader for the next element—courage.

Four: Courage

If our primary aim is to work for the good of the people, we must be prepared to show tremendous courage in the face of anything that threatens their well-being. This is particularly true when dealing with toxic forces or toxic people.

Generally speaking, that which is toxic has no ability to self-regulate. A cancer cell is a toxic force. It spreads as rapidly as it can to wherever it can. As a leader, I have personally experienced toxic people. They spread their negativity, dissatisfaction, discontent, and destruction to anyone who will listen—all for the purpose of destroying the leader or the organization.

The only way to stop a toxic force is to destroy or remove it. Cancer cells must be destroyed or removed. And when it comes to toxic forces or people in the organization, they must be stopped. In this case, a leader must courageously stand in fierce opposition to the toxic force.

I (Matt) once sat in an audience listening to former Tennessee Governor Bill Haslam discuss his perspective on leadership. A well-regarded leader himself, he suggested the role of a leader in times of challenge is to "bear the pain of the people, not inflict it upon them." There aren't many better descriptions of what leadership is than that. It takes courage to truly lead and work for the good of the people.

As we think about courage, it is appropriate for us to go back to one of the first examples from the book of Esther, the story Dr. Jackson loved to share. Esther didn't ask to be put into a leadership role. She never took business management classes or read bestselling books on guiding organizations or had a leadership coach. History even tells us that she was made queen more for her beauty than for her skills.

Regardless of how Esther ended up in a leadership role, she wound up at the crossroads of her people's destiny—and her own. She was put into an uncomfortable position where she had to make a crucial decision: risk her life by pleading her people's case before a dangerous king, or protect her position and walk away from the crisis at hand.

But she embraced the truth of Esther 4:14, which has been misquoted by countless college football coaches, players, and fans on Saturday game days: "And who knows but that you have come to your royal position for such a time as this?"

Esther asked the entire Jewish community to fast and pray with her for three days and nights before approaching the king. "And if I perish, I perish," she said, fully embracing the mantle of leadership.

Queen Esther was willing to put it all on the line—her status, her position, her comfort and stability, the perks of being a queen, even her very life—in order to do what God had called her to do. Her courage wasn't a manifestation of reckless behavior or an out-of-control ego. She simply believed that certain things are worth living—and dying—for.

When I look at the state of the world and the state of our churches, organizations, and communities today, I can't help but think that for true renewal to occur, a whole generation of leaders is going to have to rise up with the courage of Esther. We must diligently examine what it means to take the next right step, to be light in the darkness, to be set apart, more relevant, more intentional, more gracious, more loving, and more committed to working for the good of the people.

As leaders who are called to move toward the future with courage and boldness, we need to understand that doing the right thing can—and will—cost us.

I'm stepping all over my own toes on this one. I can't count how many times I've looked in the mirror or lain in bed wondering, *What am I waiting for? How long will I sit in comfort and stability while God has placed me here—now—for a purpose?* Too often I hesitate to act with courage because I know it's going to stretch me and it's going to be uncomfortable. I avoid discomfort, resist growth, and sidestep what's hard, even when I know it's right. Sometimes, as leaders, we grow complacent, apathetic in our roles, reluctant to embrace the challenge. But we are called to lead boldly, right where we are, no matter the cost.

When we catch ourselves feeling this way in our various positions of leadership, may we remember the courage of Esther, who, when faced with a choice, said, "I'll do the right thing. And if I perish, I perish."

Five: Excitement for Life

A compelling leadership presence conveys an energy that can be seen and felt. The best leaders are excited to simply be present, showing up with a smile, a bounce in their step, optimism, openness, kindness, and generosity. A leader's positive energy is contagious, spreading life equally as fast as that which is toxic spreads destruction.

The presence of a leader—good or bad—can be felt whenever they walk into a room. We're all allowed to have bad days from time to time, but there is something so impactful to the people in our care when we take the time to be intentional, to live on purpose. To lead from the Core, we must embrace the truth that we are given these positions for a reason that is bigger than ourselves. We have a responsibility to steward our organization and our people.

Effective leaders need to embrace a big-picture perspective, even when they are tired, grumpy, or just not feeling it. Being a true leader means showing up with excitement, energy, and positivity for every opportunity, knowing that each day offers the promise of purpose and meaning. We set the tone by bringing our best to the table, modeling the enthusiasm we wish to see from our teams.

This doesn't mean we should fake our way through life and never allow others to see us struggle. In fact, showing vulnerability allows you to be relationally present and available for your people. All too often, leaders fail to show the proper levels of emotion or pretend not to be bothered by challenges. But fake positivity only puts more distance between us and those we are called to lead, and often, the only ones we're fooling are ourselves.

To lead from the Core, you must toggle between the big-picture perspective and the emotion of the moment. Our ability and willingness to acknowledge that things aren't quite right allows us to be seen as real people by our followers and can create a stronger sense of trust and unity. While we can acknowledge the very real feelings of frustration, discouragement, and disappointment, we should call ourselves—and our people—to remember the larger vision. And we need to be able to do this in a way that is winsome and not sarcastic or off-putting.

We hope the work you're doing is meaningful enough to tap into a natural reservoir of adrenaline—fueling the energy and excitement your team needs from you. But if your current efforts don't feel especially meaningful, we hope you're still driven by a deeper sense of purpose or a dream to do or become more. That inner fire matters. Whether it comes from the mission itself or your personal vision, your passion is essential to move your organization from where it is to where it needs to be.

Presence under Pressure

Leadership presence is not a performance—it's a practice. It's not about delivering a flawless message or mastering the latest framework. It's about embodying character, humility, self-awareness, restraint, and courage, especially when the spotlight fades and the pressure mounts. Anyone can lead when times are good. It's how you show up when things are uncertain, messy, or broken that defines your influence. The leader in our opening story didn't fail because she lacked intelligence. She failed because she lost her connection to her people. She lost her ability to have grace under pressure. And when grace disappears, trust is the next thing to go.

Graceful leadership doesn't mean being passive or avoiding hard truths. Quite the opposite! Grace allows you to say and do hard things in the right way. It demands we confront toxic behavior while preserving human dignity. It invites honesty about our own limitations while still leading with strength. Grace is not weakness. It's strength under control.

What does your leadership presence say about you? When your team sees you walk into the room—on your best days and on your worst—do they feel steadied or stirred? Encouraged or afraid? The legacy you leave will not be shaped by what you said in a keynote or posted on your bio but by how you showed up day after day, especially when it counted most. Show up with grace, and you will not only build trust—you'll build people. And that's the kind of leadership the world needs now more than ever.

CHAPTER 20

Pace Yourself and Extend the Game

Most people can vividly recall where they were and what they were doing in March 2020 when our world shut down due to the coronavirus pandemic. I (Matt) was in a senior leadership roll at a university. Like many sectors, higher ed was tumultuous, especially in those first two years of the pandemic. Every morning, it felt like we were being hit with a tsunami of information and anxieties, forced to make yet more demanding decisions.

A study by the American Council on Education found that the average tenure of a college president decreased from 8.5 years in 2006 to 5.9 years in 2022, in large part due to the challenges of Covid.*

---

* Danielle Douglas-Gabriel, "The Wave of College Presidential Departures Hits HBCUs," *The Washington Post*, September 2, 2023, https://www.washingtonpost.com/education/2023/09/02/hbcu-president-departures/.

Another study found that over 40 percent of US clergy have seriously contemplated leaving their congregations since 2020, with more than half considering exiting ministry altogether.*

Leaders, like everyone else affected by the pandemic, were exhausted.

At our university, it seemed we were navigating the pandemic moment by moment, doing our best to serve students, calm parents, and appease stakeholders. We suspected that if we pivoted to 100 percent online learning, much of our constituency would have opted out. So we decided that coming back to school in-person in the fall of 2020 was imperative—we just didn't know what that would look like.

We worked countless hours to put policies and guidelines in place, avoiding the political overtones as best we could. We turned one dorm into a quarantine space. Planning for all scenarios, we created a process for determining how students would be transported to the doctor, who would assist them, and how long they'd be in quarantine. If one pocket of students got infected, the virus would spread fast. And if that happened, we knew that the city would shut us down.

Throughout those precarious days in fall 2020, I would often repeat this mantra to my team: "Pace yourself and extend the game." I'm a big sports guy, and I drew this piece of wisdom from the game of basketball.

Picture this: You're down by five points with a minute to go in the game. You don't just let the clock run out. You extend the game. You

---

* Peter Smith, "U.S. Pastors Struggle with Post-Pandemic Burnout; Survey Shows Many Have Considered Quitting," *Associated Press*, January 11, 2024, https://apnews.com/article/christian-clergy-burnout-pandemic-survey-24ee46327438ff46b074d234ffe2f58c

foul. You hope the other team misses their free throws. You full-court press. You foul again. Maybe they make one out of two free throws. Then on your next possession, you hit a three.

Suddenly, you're right back in it with thirty seconds to go. And so you foul again. You do everything you can to stretch out those final moments. That's extending the game. It's also your job as a leader: Set the pace and extend the game. Manage yourself and your team so you can stay in the competition—and eventually get the win.

This leadership skill came into sharp focus during the pandemic. Leaders were forced to reckon with decisions that would make or break their organizations—and themselves. At our university, we put measures in place to extend the game. We told ourselves, *If we can just make it through one hundred days—if we can get to Thanksgiving—we'll be okay.*

I remember that countdown vividly. We planned for students to go home after Thanksgiving. Finals would be remote, and no one would return until January. That was the strategy—extend the game, protect the community, and live to fight another semester.

And guess what? It worked. We remained afloat, and today the school is thriving.

The question arises: *How* do we do this? The best way to pace yourself and extend the game comes from a transformational teaching I heard from none other than Dr. Ken Jones, many years ago.

Cutting Through the Fog

In the story of Clint and Dr. Jackson, you heard them reference "the fog" several times. It might seem like a strange concept for a leadership book, but upon closer examination, every leader will immediately resonate with this concept. I (Ken) am speaking of a mental fog—the kind that grows so dense in one's mind that it clouds your vision of everything else in life.

I suspect you have been there many times. Typically, it's a problem we wrestle with for long stretches of time. And the longer we wrestle with it, the deeper the fog becomes. As the fog becomes denser, all hope for clarity evaporates. Even falling asleep is difficult as your mind races and refuses to shut down. Or, even if you are able to fall asleep with relative ease, you wake up in the middle of the night, the problem still at the forefront of your mind. And you still have no answer.

Does this sound familiar?

Leaders must quickly recognize the fog and have the tools to deal with it. Why? Because the fog is so dangerous. As it deepens, the one who's stuck in it becomes more and more desperate, and a state of desperation leads to flirting with things you'd never normally entertain.

We've all heard of employees suddenly quitting their jobs with no place to go. Husbands or wives walking away from marriages that seemed picture-perfect on the outside. People who seemed like they'd be immune to addiction reaching for alcohol or drugs. Those we consider our heroes committing moral failures—embezzlement, affairs, abuse, fraud. People will do desperate things when they've been caught in the fog for a long time.

What causes the fog? It begins when a leader is caught in an unrelenting season of fatigue. The fog sets in, and flirtation follows. The fog leads to such a desperate state that the leader begins flirting with a thought that leads to an action that, under normal circumstances, they would never even entertain.

In early 2025, I (Matt) received an email from a business leader I had met before but did not know well, asking if we could visit about his company and some of the opportunities he saw for it. The man, a brilliant, highly educated, very successful entrepreneur, and I were able to talk by phone the next day to set up a time to meet a couple of days later. In that initial phone call, he told me that he felt it was time to put some new emphasis on a piece of his company that, while successful, could do even better with some new ideas and strategies. On the phone, he seemed positive and ready to create a new future for that part of his business. I looked forward to meeting with him a few days later.

The very next morning, while sitting in a meeting with another client, I received a call from the man. He left me a voicemail, and as soon as I had a chance to listen, I heard him say something like this, "Matt, I know we are supposed to meet tomorrow about how to grow that part of my business, but I had some stuff come up this morning and I think I might just sell it. Not sure if we need to meet tomorrow or not. Call me if you get a chance." I was intrigued to say the least. The positive tone I sensed from him less than twenty-four hours before now seemed to be replaced with negativity and despair.

I called him immediately and began to listen to him describe what had transpired that morning. He started by telling me that early that morning, his longest tenured employee, the person he felt was the glue to that part of his business, had told him she was moving to another part of the country for family reasons. He went on to say that if she wasn't going to be involved, his business had no hope of functioning well, let alone being prepared to grow and move in new directions. To say he was shook up is an understatement. I listened as he described her work ethic, her talent, and just how much of the business he had put in her hands.

I first tried to empathize with him, remembering I did not know him well and we hadn't really even started discussing his business and all of its nuances at this point, so I felt like I was playing "catch up" from the onset of the phone call. The first question that popped into my head was, "How long did she give you before she will be leaving?" His response stunned me a bit. He said, "Seven months." I remember thinking to myself, *Seven months?! Are you kidding me? We can recover and come up with a plan for all of this*. I am glad I didn't say that out loud.

I did, however, think to ask this question: "Why do you feel like this is something you and your business can't navigate?" It was then that he said the words that would become the basis for our subsequent conversations over the next several months.

He said, "Matt, I am so tired. I have been trying to figure out what to do with this company for a long time. I feel stuck and am not sure what to do with any of it."

We visited for a few more minutes and then told him we definitely needed to keep our appointment the next afternoon. The following day, we met for a couple of hours in a quiet corner of a restaurant. He seemed to feel a little better after having had some time to collect his thoughts. We began to unpack all that was going on, and as he described not only the business situation he now found himself in but the last several years of stops and starts with new ideas and strategies, he began to unravel just how fatigued he had become with decision making, employee challenges, shifting markets, and how all of those things crept in as he thought about his own legacy and potential exit planning down the road. The state he found himself in on that day was no longer tolerable for him. He sat there, full of business intellect and expertise, but caught up in a fatigue-infused fog that was so thick, he was flirting with decisions even he in that moment knew didn't make sense.

Toward the end of that first conversation, I told him two things. The first was that I encouraged him not to make any major business-related decisions for the next thirty days. He understood the need to not jump into anything that would short-circuit the business that he had built. The second thing was this: I said, "You reached out to discuss some strategic planning for the future, and we can help do that, but I think before we do any of that, my first task is to help you cut through the fog you find yourself in." I went on to describe the relationship between fatigue, fog, and the flirtation it can lead to, and he agreed that was where we needed to start.

Several months later, the man's business is doing as well or better than it had in many years, and he seems to be thriving. We continue to meet and discuss a lot of items related to his leadership and his business, but we always check in on the fog and its impact on him. He recently introduced me to a business colleague, and it did my heart good to hear him say, "This is Matt. He helps people like us get unstuck and cut through the fog." I was glad to hear it, humbled to be a part of a journey that many leaders need to take: the journey to pace ourselves and extend the game.

The Three Types of Fatigue

No one is exempt from getting tired, which means no one is exempt from the brutal combination of fog and flirtation. To keep ourselves out of this dangerous place, we must first understand what causes fatigue.

Fatigue comes from three sources: physical, emotional, and spiritual. Each of us possesses energy in these three reservoirs. When any one or more of these becomes low or depleted, we become fatigued.

Three Energy Reservoirs

Physical   Emotional   Spiritual

Physical Fatigue

Physical fatigue is often the first sign of exhaustion we notice. Our body is always sending us signals about the state of our inner reservoir. But whether we listen to it or not is a different matter.

At this very moment, how would you rate your physical energy on a scale from 1 to 10? Do you feel tension or pain? Do you feel alert and engaged? What is your body telling you about the state of your physical well-being?

Here's another exercise for you: Pause and make a list of all the things in your life that contribute to a depletion of your physical energy. What's on your list? I suspect poor diet, lack of sleep, working too many hours, stress, and no regular exercise may be common entries. We each know what it's like to become physically tired. Bringing awareness to the state of our bodies is the first step in cutting out the fog and avoiding flirtation. The Bible addresses this in 1 Corinthians 6:19–20: "Do you not know that your bodies are temples of the Holy Spirit, who is in you, whom you have from God? You are not your own; you were bought at a price. Therefore honor God with your bodies."

Emotional Fatigue

Emotional fatigue is as common as physical fatigue, but it's often harder to describe and quantify. Pause again and make a list of things you have experienced or witnessed that cause emotional energy depletion. This time, your list probably contains phrases of explanation. If you were to categorize the phrases you have written, they would probably fall under a few main categories: life changes, relationship problems, and fear.

Life changes are often positive. Some of life's best moments lie just on the other side of change—a wedding, a new job, a move to a new area. But preparing for such an event and carrying it through often depletes our reservoir. I witnessed this truth when my daughter got married. She and my wife planned the event for months. It was a December "Christmas"-themed wedding. The thousands of details, the organizing, the decisions, and the sheer fact that our daughter was leaving our home and bringing into our family a new member we so greatly loved—it was all-consuming. When the wedding day was over, Suz and I were absolutely exhausted. Part of the exhaustion was physical, but most of it was emotional.

Relationship problems are another major source of emotional drain. If you have a substantial argument with your spouse and then go off to work, at every free moment, where does your mind go? Yes, it goes right back to the fight as you worry about how to fix it. And if the fighting has been going on for a long time, to the point where you wonder if your marriage will last, it's almost impossible to spare enough emotional energy needed for your work.

The last category is fear, which takes a nearly infinite number of shapes. Fear could arise when you're employed by an organization that is struggling financially. You're constantly worrying about whether the company will make it or whether your job is secure. In the meantime, you're being asked to do more work with fewer resources, take on additional responsibilities, and do it all with a positive attitude.

The more out of control we feel, the bigger our fears become. Receiving news of a major illness, a financial collapse that robs your retirement savings, or a boss deciding to downsize and eliminate your job are all examples of events that are out of our control. There is nothing we can do, and fear and helplessness are the result. Our emotional energy is spent worrying about the situation instead of accomplishing anything productive.

Spiritual Fatigue

The third energy reservoir each of us possesses is spiritual. This reservoir is a bit harder to pinpoint because, to some, the entire subject of spirituality is taboo and the concept is hard to grasp. Plus, the word itself carries different meanings for different people. For our purposes, perhaps the best definition of *spiritual* is "having a connection to a higher power." For me, that means having a connection to a God who I believe created the universe and with whom I have a deep relationship. Being "spiritual" means I believe I am loved, watched over, and protected by God. I understand you may have your own definition or experience of the word.

When we are disconnected from this source of higher power, our spiritual reservoir is drained. The disconnect comes when we believe we are completely self-sufficient, not requiring help from anything or anyone. But none of us can do life by ourselves. If we think we can, we're being prideful, and having that attitude will completely destroy our spiritual tanks. Those with an ego out of control, as we discussed earlier, are especially susceptible to depleting their spiritual energy.

We weren't designed to grow and produce by ourselves. Our spiritual tanks are filled through praying, studying Scripture, reflecting, visiting with other people, listening to teachers, fasting, meditating, and other spiritual disciplines. They are emptied simply by ignoring all of these actions.

To summarize, we have three basic energy reservoirs within us: physical, emotional, and spiritual. Depletion of energy in any one or more of these tanks yields fatigue. And fatigue leads to getting stuck in a mental fog, which can lead to flirtation with dangerous behavior.

Elijah's Exhaustion

The best illustration I know of the three tanks being depleted comes from Scripture.

The story is from the life of a man named Elijah, who is somewhat of a superhero of the Old Testament. God sent Elijah to speak to the king of Israel, a man named Ahab. Ahab was a selfish, spoiled, dangerous, and bad king. To make matters worse, his wife, Jezebel, was more selfish and wicked than he was. The two together made quite a pair.

Elijah went to Ahab and announced that there would be a major drought in the land. Despite the wrath he was sure to encounter from the wicked king, Elijah trusted God and boldly proclaimed the truth. Then he went into hiding for some time. Three years passed, bringing devastation to the land. Ahab was so angry that he sent soldiers everywhere trying to find Elijah so that he might kill him. And at such a time as this, God gave Elijah another command: "Go back and confront Ahab. Tell him the drought is all his wicked fault."

Elijah was strong in his faith. He went.

The place where Elijah met Ahab was a mountain called Carmel, where a "showdown" of sorts was about to take place between Ahab's god, Baal, and Elijah's God, Yahweh. Elijah proposed a test to prove which of the gods was true. Two altars would be built, with a calf placed on each altar. The prophets of Baal would call on their god, and Elijah would call on his God. The one who answered with fire and consumed what was on the altar would be recognized as the one true God.

Everyone agreed to the test, and the prophets of Baal went first. They built their altar and placed the calf upon it. Then they began to call on their god, but they received no answer. Elijah taunted them, calling out, "Is he asleep?" After hours of summoning their unresponsive god, the prophets of Baal became upset and exhausted, and they gave up.

Now it was Elijah's turn. He took twelve stones and placed them as the foundation for his altar. Then he arranged the wood on the stones. The calf was then placed in pieces on the altar. And then Elijah went a step further, perhaps for a bit of drama. He dug a trench around the altar. Then he had others bring water jars and drench the calf with water. He didn't do it just once, but three times. Water ran off the altar and filled the trench.

When Elijah called on his God, a fire roared down from heaven, consuming the calf, the wood, the stones, and the water! The people needed no more convincing. Everybody was now on Elijah's side—and on the side of his God.

But the day was not over yet. Elijah took control of the mountainside and ordered the 450 prophets of Baal to be gathered. He took them to the valley and killed them all, an act that surely took an unimaginable emotional toll. Elijah then climbed to the top of the mountain and began to beg God to send rain. He spent a long time doing this, begging God a total of seven times for rain.

Finally, Elijah saw a small cloud appear and knew it was going to rain. He sent word to Ahab to return home, for the rain was coming. Elijah then ran all the way to where Ahab would be. Some say the distance was a marathon length of twenty-six miles.

Taunting, killing, climbing a mountain, begging God, running a long distance—Elijah was physically and emotionally empty. But what about spiritually? He'd had a mountaintop experience, so the assumption is he must have been very full spiritually. The story, at this point, illustrates what happens in all our lives. The speed, clutter, and demands of life can quickly empty one or more of our tanks. When it does, the fatigue leads to fog, and the fog leads to flirtation with behaviors we normally would never consider.

The story of Elijah continues. Ahab, who was at home, told Jezebel all that had happened. Furious, she sent a message to Elijah, telling him, "By this time tomorrow, I will make sure you are dead just like my prophets." What happened next needs careful attention and consideration. The story says Elijah was afraid.

What?

That doesn't sound like the reaction of a strong man of faith. But it was true. In his fear, Elijah ran for his life. That doesn't sound like the Elijah we know, does it? But there's more. In the next part of the story, Elijah is described as standing under a tree, wishing he were dead.

These are behaviors no one would have ever dreamed of from a man who had experienced so much of God's power. But the fog had overtaken him. And desperation and discouragement loomed out of the fog, causing Elijah to flirt with behavior that was not normal.

Protecting Your People from the Fog

If we are to work for the good of the people, we must protect ourselves from the fog and those we lead as well. If we are not careful, our decisions will be the source of their fatigue.

I know of an organization that hosts an annual event for its most loyal customers. It takes a great deal of planning and coordination to pull off. The small team responsible for organizing the event already carries a full load of complex, demanding daily responsibilities. Still, when their CEO "voluntold" (yes, that's a thing) them to serve on the planning committee, they agreed—motivated by love for their customers and a servant's heart.

The day of the big event arrived, and like previous years, it was a huge success. The event ran late into the night, and though the team was exhausted, they stayed until the end, proud of what they had accomplished. The CEO—who received most of the credit and enjoyed the spotlight—spent a few minutes with the tired team near the end of the evening, already brainstorming ideas for next year. As you can imagine, the eye rolls and smirks were hard to hide, but everyone smiled politely, wrapped things up, and began cleanup, knowing full well that their regular work would resume early the next morning.

Still tired and a bit frustrated by the CEO's lack of awareness, the team awoke the next day feeling some satisfaction that the event had gone well and was now over. That feeling quickly faded when one of the team members checked her email, then urged the others to do the same.

Waiting in their inbox was an email the CEO had sent at 6 a.m. The team had hoped for a simple thank-you—and maybe a well-earned day off. Instead, they found a document outlining ways they could improve in their day jobs, along with an invitation to a long meeting the next day to discuss the potential changes.

Unsurprisingly, this didn't go over well. Already running on empty, the team felt unseen and unappreciated. The fog of burnout only thickened. Some members quit outright; others quit emotionally but stayed at the company, stuck in a fog that would linger.

All of this was caused by a single early morning email—likely sent just to check a box on the CEO's to-do list. The damage it caused was almost impossible to measure.

Avoiding Fatigue, Fog, and Flirtation

If we are, as Matt said, to "pace ourselves and extend the game," how are we to avoid the fatigue that leads to a treacherous outcome? Below are a few pieces of wisdom I've gained from my own life and from coaching leaders over the years.

Respect Your Rhythms and Limits

As leaders, we must pay close attention to the rhythms and routines that shape our lives. Many of us are naturally competitive and driven, which makes it easy to take on more responsibility and activity than is healthy. But the wear and tear on both body and spirit is real. Saying no is a challenge for many leaders. We often see saying no as a weakness—or worse, as failing to live up to some unspoken badge of honor that comes with leadership.

We don't want to appear vulnerable, so we build unsustainable rhythms into our lives—patterns that quietly tear us apart. And these patterns don't just affect us. They inevitably spill over onto the people we love the most. This has been a personal struggle for me throughout my leadership journey. Even now, as I write these words, I find myself in the early stages of trying to reset. I'm sitting on the deck of a tiny cabin near a lake—not just to write but to rest, to recharge, and to become more of the person I need to be for those I love and lead.

If we're going to lead well over the long haul, we must find ways to reconnect—especially spiritually. The work we do, and the people we serve, depends on it. Rest is not a luxury. It's a discipline, a lifeline, a sacred rhythm that allows us to function from overflow rather than exhaustion.

We cannot give what we haven't cultivated within ourselves. That starts with honest reflection, courageous choices, and a commitment to rhythms that restore, not deplete. It starts, quite literally, with stopping.

Keep Your Tanks Full

Fatigue sets in when our tanks are depleted. As long as we're keeping those tanks full, we will avoid the slide into exhaustion.

Keeping the physical tank full is usually straightforward: rest, sleep, good nutrition, exercise, and vacation. I love what happens to Elijah in this regard. While he's under a tree, afraid and discouraged to the point of wanting to die, he falls asleep. After a while, he feels a tap on his shoulder. An angel has prepared hot bread and brought him a jar of water. He eats, drinks, and goes back to sleep. Sometimes the most spiritual thing a leader can do is take care of the basic needs of their body.

Protecting the emotional tank, however, is much harder. In 2010, I joined a yearlong leadership and coaching program in Dallas led by author, teacher, and clinical psychologist Dr. John Townsend. I applied because I was worn out—maybe even burned out—from prolonged stress. About a year earlier, I'd realized something was off. I couldn't sleep. I was anxious. I wanted out of my job. Something needed to change.

I got into the program, and about three months in, I got a call from Dr. Townsend on a Saturday morning—something I wasn't expecting. I had been teaching the "three tanks" concept for years, but I never truly understood how to refill the emotional tank. That changed in one thirty-minute phone call.

Dr. Townsend started by saying, "Ken, I've got you figured out." That's not what you want to hear from a psychologist! He said I was a classic CEO type: constantly giving but never letting anyone get close. He explained that all this giving without receiving was leaving me drained, anxious, and empty. I agreed.

Then he said something that really shook me: "I don't know your wife. I've only met her briefly. But I bet you're killing her. You come home every day and dump everything on her because you don't talk to anyone else. I'd guess she's just as worn out as you are."

Again, he was right.

Then came another bold statement: "Ken, I can fix you."

I laughed and asked, "How?"

That's when he introduced a concept I'd never heard about before: *relational energy*. He explained that relational energy is the key to refilling the emotional tank—and keeping it from running dry in the first place. Then Dr. Townsend gave me an assignment: Find at least two "safe" people—individuals I could trust completely, who wouldn't judge me or betray my confidence. People who could handle the truth about how I was doing without flinching or fixing. He told me to meet with them regularly—every three weeks or so—and just be honest with them, sharing my frustrations, failures, and fears and letting the real me be known.

It wasn't easy at first. Vulnerability doesn't come naturally to me. But I did it. I found two people. I started sharing. And something incredible happened—I began to feel stronger. Over time, I felt restored, lighter, and more grounded. Those relationships began to refill me emotionally. To this day, I still meet with those people. That practice has become essential to my well-being.

Relational energy is the most reliable way I've found to keep my emotional tank full. You saw Dr. Jackson live this out in front of his young intern when he took the coaching call from his executive coach, Michael. We never outgrow our need for relational energy.

Now, a final word about the spiritual tank. Earlier, I used the word *connection* to describe the spiritual life. I'll say it more plainly now: I believe in God—the same God Elijah cried out to under the tree. Over time, I'm learning to trust him more fully, to let him into every corner of my life.

I take intentional steps to keep my connection with God alive because I know what happens when I lose it. When I try to do life on my own, I get overwhelmed quickly. But when I stay connected—through prayer, Scripture, silence, worship, and community—I find strength I don't possess on my own.

My encouragement to you is this: Believe in something bigger than yourself. Lean into your faith and be strong in the hope and the rest that come from the almighty God. That is the only way to keep your spiritual tank full. And if the three tanks are key to sustaining leadership, then the spiritual tank is the anchor. It's what holds the other two tanks in place.

Extend the Game of Life

Many leaders thrive in crisis situations. But this idea of pacing yourself and extending the game goes far beyond short-term sprints. It's a marathon mindset.

"Pace yourself and extend the game" applies in the short term—getting your team through a season, a sprint, a challenge. And it applies long term as well—navigating succession, building something sustainable, finishing well. As leaders, if we don't pace ourselves and manage our energy, we will crash and burn. And we'll burn our organizations down with us. We'll wreck our health and our relationships. We may end up as another cautionary tale about "moral failure."

Pacing yourself and extending the game applies to every area of your life. You can extend the game at work, but if your marriage falls apart or your kids don't want to come home for college breaks, what's the point? You've got to extend the game in your marriage, in your parenting, in your health—so you can keep showing up and working with purpose.

For the hard-driving types reading this—the ones who say, "Forget self-care! I'll sleep when I'm dead!"—we hope this perspective gives you a new lens. It's not about taking a day off just for the fun of it. Taking care of yourself is not an escape. Sometimes it takes a global pandemic to cause us to pause and reestablish our routines and rhythms, but I hope for those seeking to lead from the Core, it can become a regular, intentional discipline to pause, reset, take a deep breath, and move forward more sustainably. It is a strategy to stay in the game longer and maximize your impact while keeping your eye on the mission ahead.

Be Coachable

I (Matt) caught the basketball bug early in life, and it played a tremendous role not only in my upbringing but also in my development as a leader. Nothing beats the role sports can play in teaching kids about life, teamwork, resiliency, hard work, and discipline. I took pride in playing the "right" way, so as not to let my team down. Over the years, I soaked up all the basketball knowledge I could, thinking I wanted to be a coach one day. I loved it when people referred to me as a "coach on the court."

Basketball also provided a way for me to continue my education after high school. While Duke, Kentucky, Kansas, and other big-name schools apparently did not need my slow-footed services, I did receive a scholarship to play at a small Christian college, and I was grateful for the opportunity. It meant a lot to my family for me to be able to attend a good school and play ball at the same time.

Throughout my college career, I had the pleasure of learning from a variety of leaders, many of them on the court. Our head coach would occasionally allow visiting coaches or friends who were in between coaching jobs to talk to our team or run us through some favorite drills.

One of our guest coaches had enjoyed a successful stint as a small-college coach before taking on a Division I head coaching role. He stopped by often to work with us, but one day stands out in my memory. He was putting us through a new drill. I loved learning new drills. In fact, with all my young adult knowledge and wisdom, I'd been thinking we needed to spruce things up and had a list of some good drills to recommend if our coach ever decided to seek out my opinion.

The starting five tried to execute the new drill the guest coach taught us, but we completely messed it up. The guest coach corrected them and had them repeat the drill. They messed it up again. Then the second string tried it, but somehow they messed it up as well. The guest coach had grown weary of our team's inability to pick up this new drill, so he stopped everything and went back through each step, drilling the steps into our thick heads. We could sense the growing frustration in his voice.

As a redshirt freshman, I sat at the end of the bench with a few of my teammates. We were the last line of players to run through things. I liked going third, as it gave me a chance to see what I was supposed to be doing before I attempted it. But as soon as the guest coach walked us through the drill, he didn't call for the starters to get back out there—he called on the bench. That wasn't ideal for me. I was still confused, but I didn't want to let on that I hadn't been paying close attention during the second explanation.

I ran down the court and completely botched the drill.

I have been scolded many times, but rarely have I received a tongue-lashing quite like that one. The guest coach pulled me aside and let me have it. He couldn't believe my lack of attention or desire to improve. "Matt," he said, "you are uncoachable!"

I remember those words like it was yesterday. They stung deeply. I'd always prided myself on being a "coach on the floor," for "doing things the right way." Did he not know who I was? Did he not understand I was a rule follower, someone who received straight A's in class and never missed a university chapel program? Who was he to say that I was uncoachable?

I could see the relief in my teammates' eyes that it was me and not them experiencing the wrath of the guest coach.

The exchange felt like it lasted an eternity, but eventually, we got back to practice.

Later that night back in my dorm room, I tried to be reflective—or at least as reflective as a nineteen-year-old college student can be. I admitted to myself that the guest coach's words held some truth. At times, I *was* uncoachable—for a few reasons.

The first reason was that I already had all the answers—or at least, I thought I did. This pride led me to the second reason: I refused to ask for help when I needed it. I felt a pit in my stomach as I thought through what had happened that day, but also about other moments in my life where my ego had gotten in the way of my willingness to show a level of vulnerability or coachability.

Things eventually improved between that coach and me. He returned to full-time coaching, and I became a coach at my alma mater. Eventually, we even shared a laugh about that day and that drill. He went on to gain national recognition, guiding teams to impressive March Madness runs. Watching his teams play with such toughness—and hearing commentators praise him for it—I often wondered if his players had ever been challenged to be more coachable. I've remained grateful for the pivotal lesson I learned that day, one I've carried throughout my life and career.

Being Coachable

To lead from the Core, one must be coachable—just as Clint was open to Dr. Jackson's mentorship. But what does coachability look like beyond the world of sports?

It begins with a concept we discussed earlier in this book: a genuine sense of humility. Humility helps us keep our ego in check, as we discussed in chapter sixteen. It allows us to remain eager to learn and helps us commit to having a growth mindset. When we admit we don't have all the answers, a whole world of wisdom opens to us. Humble people tend to be wise people, because they recognize their need for guidance.

We should all strive to be people who seek wisdom—not just knowledge but true and lasting wisdom. The concept of wisdom is praised in the ancient book of Proverbs. Here are just a few examples:

> "Listen to my instruction and be wise; do not disregard it"
> (Proverbs 8:33).

"Mockers resent correction, so they avoid the wise"
(Proverbs 15:12).

"Listen to advice and accept discipline, and at the end you will be counted among the wise" (Proverbs 19:20).

Wisdom is a gift, and pride keeps us from receiving this gift we all desperately need if we want to truly lead from the Core. In the book *Boundaries*, we read, "Wisdom is not something we know; it's something we do. Only when we allow God to give us teachable hearts will he show us what we need to know in order to help us change what we do. The biggest fool of all is the person who knows from God what to do and who won't do it. That person is not teachable."

Here, we must pause for a moment of self-reflection. Are we teachable and open to the pursuit of wisdom? And if we think we are, how can we know for sure? After all, pride blinds us. If you're wondering where you stand, let's see how the following prompts resonate with you:

- Are people willing to tell you things you need to hear, even if they're challenging? If so, you are likely coachable.
- When confronted or called out by others who are genuinely concerned about you, have you taken their advice or insights to heart and taken positive actions? If not, you may have a coachability problem.
- Do you ever get defensive when people try to offer you instruction or advice? If so, you may not have the growth mindset necessary to be coachable.
- Do you often feel the need to "return the teaching" when someone corrects you? If so, you may be uncoachable.

- Have people been sharing the same advice with you for many years? If so, it might be time to consider that a coachable person would have made progress in those areas instead of just continuing to deal with the same old issues.

These questions are only a starting point for personal reflection. To take your assessment a step further, ask friends, colleagues, or family members you trust to offer their perspective on your level of willingness to learn. Be prepared for some hard truths—not everything they have to say will be easy to hear.

There's an old Chinese proverb that says, "A man who asks is a fool for five minutes. A man who never asks is a fool for life." Be willing to look like a fool now to save yourself the heartache later.

Coachability and Listening

It is difficult not to notice how this principle overlaps with another Core leadership principle—that of leading with our ears. Leading with your ears helps you pay attention to the problems and needs of your people. It also keeps you open to honest feedback, advice, and wisdom when you need coaching. You cannot learn unless you're first willing to listen, especially to those in your closest circles of trust who want to help you be the best version of yourself you can be.

Choosing to listen and open yourself up to feedback requires vulnerability. Some may find it confusing or even off-putting to speak of the word *vulnerability* in the same book that covers some of the "stronger" aspects of leadership—like courage, vision, and presence. I get it. Many people, especially those in leadership roles, do not like the idea of being seen as vulnerable.

But the type of vulnerability I'm discussing here is not that which makes us weak or timid. As we lead from the Core, being vulnerable means choosing a posture of humility and demonstrating a willingness to learn. Our openness gives our followers a sense of hope for the wise and forward-thinking strength that comes from being a leader who is eager to learn from the talents, gifts, experiences, and expertise of those around them.

Be willing to pay close attention when life hands you a lesson, even when it may take you out of your comfort zone. Strive to be coachable so you can continue to move yourself, your people, and your organization forward.

Looking for Coachable Moments

I (Ken) have coached and been coached over many years. One of the foundational truths I've learned is that in order for coaching to work, a person has to *want* to be coached. If you, as the CEO, tell someone on your team, "You need to get some coaching," but that person doesn't *want* to be coached, you're wasting your time.

My most successful coaching experiences have come when someone said, "I'm miserable" or "I don't know what I want to do" or "I feel lost." When someone is genuinely seeking help, you can walk with them—asking good questions—and help them get to a new place. On the other hand, when a coaching client comes to the first few conversations with a prideful or negative attitude, there is a much stronger likelihood our sessions will not go in the intended direction. I learned a while back that when I sense disinterest from a coaching client, especially when their employer is the one who has paid for the coaching sessions, I quickly move to the following question: "Do you consider yourself to be coachable?" Their answer to that question usually determines if I am willing to take them on as a coaching client or not.

I've recently been coaching a leader with a PhD in physical therapy who is in charge of a strong academic program at a public university in Arkansas. As we talked, she began opening up about some leadership challenges she was facing with the department heads above her in the organizational structure. The situation was wearing her down and making her life miserable.

I decided to employ one of my favorite coaching tactics. When I sense someone is in an overwhelming and stressful situation, I'll ask, "Can you keep this up for another year?" And almost every time, they'll say, "Yes, I can do it for another year."

But then I ask, "Can you do it for five years?" That's when they pause: "No . . . I can't do this for five years."

This is what the PhD told me: "I can't keep doing this." This was the moment when it became clear that she absolutely could not continue in her current job—it was unsustainable.

The byproduct of unsustainability is always chaos. When I'm able to pinpoint this in a coaching session, I ask, "Where is the chaos showing up in your life?"

Often, especially with men, there's an initial response of: "I'm fine. I'm good." But then I'll start asking more specific questions: "How are you sleeping? How's your relationship with your spouse? How are things with your kids? Are you showing up for ball games? What's slipping through the cracks?" Eventually, they throw up their hands and say, "Okay, I get it. It's not sustainable." The chaos has become too great to ignore.

We humans are subject to an inverse relationship between emotion and intellect. When emotions go up, intellect tends to go down. For example, nobody makes their smartest decisions when they're in a rage, or struggling with deep depression, or overwhelmed by jealousy. Sometimes people get so caught up in their emotions, it's like they're caught in the fog. When someone you're coaching is stuck there, if you can help bring them out of that emotional fog and guide them back to clear thinking, you'll be much more likely to spark change.

Asking questions like "What do you really think about this?" or "What would that look like for you?" or "How would you feel if this changed?" helps people reengage both their head and their heart. Once they see their situation clearly, they can make better decisions. Some of the most coachable moments happen when someone comes face-to-face with the fact that their current way of living in chaos simply won't work long term.

The leader I was coaching had certainly reached a moment of clarity. I knew it was time to invite her to confront her situation, so I asked, "What do you want to do about it? What are the next steps?" When she admitted that her unsustainable life was creating overwhelming chaos, new options began to emerge, and she began to see a path visible through the fog.

I asked her, "What would it be like if you had the opportunity to take a new role, maybe in a new city?"

She was silent for a moment before responding, "I'd have to talk to my husband and really think about that."

Three weeks later, she's now interviewing for a high-level position just down the road at the University of Oklahoma—and chances are, she's going to be offered the job, accept it, and move to a new city and embrace a new challenge. Her breakthrough coaching moment came when she realized that the byproduct of unsustainability is always chaos. When someone hits that breaking point—that moment when it seems things just can't keep going the way they have been—it opens the door for real change.

Leading Starts with Learning

The legendary University of Tennessee women's basketball coach Pat Summitt once said, "The most important quality a player can have is being coachable. It's not how much you know; it's how much you're willing to learn."

The same is true of leaders. Every one of us will face moments where the limits of our own wisdom are made painfully clear—when we botch the drill, so to speak, or when the chaos of an unsustainable life starts to take its toll. These moments can either harden us or humble us. The difference lies in whether we're willing to be coached.

As leaders, teammates, parents, or friends, the invitation is the same: to remain teachable. Coachability is what keeps us growing, connected, and grounded in reality. It's what allows us to lead not just from a place of authority but from the Core—where authenticity, integrity, and transformation reside.

Ask yourself: *Where am I resisting correction? Where am I pretending to be fine when the truth is, I'm actually not okay? Who do I need to invite into my life to help me see what I can't see on my own?*

BE COACHABLE

The great leaders—the wise ones, the ones we admire most—never stop learning. May we follow their example. May we choose humility over pride, clarity over chaos, and growth over comfort. Because when we remain coachable, we remain changeable—and when we are changeable, anything is possible.

Chapter 22

Know Where You're Going and Why

My (Matt's) grandfather was an incredibly influential person during his time on earth. He impacted many people across the world through his work as a minister and church builder. Long after his passing, I can still recall many of the lessons he lived out and shared with me and others.

One of the most memorable lessons he taught me was often repeated throughout my adolescence and adult years: "Matt, there are two great days in your life: the day you are born, and the day you realize why you were born." (I hope this rings a bell from our story about Dr. Jackson and Clint!) I now know this quote was first said by theologian William Barclay, but for many years I thought it was made up by my grandpa!

I heard these words many times before they really sank in. After graduating from college, I visited my grandpa to help him move some book boxes and furniture around in his home office. While we were taking a break from the work, we began talking about this famous quote of his. Maybe it was the season of life I was in—right on the brink of entering the professional world—or maybe it was his declining health and the resulting challenges he was facing, but as we sat together that afternoon, I was finally ready to receive his wisdom.

My grandpa told me to never take for granted the importance of the first "great day." It represented the starting point for how our God-given talents, strengths, gifts, and abilities will take shape and come alive. He then went on to discuss the "second great day"—the day we realize *why* we are born. My aging and ailing grandfather wanted me to understand that we are created to use our unique talents for a unique purpose. The second great day represents the larger mission we are called to—the difference we are to make in the world.

Decades later, I started a company and named it Great Days Leadership. Our mission is to help leaders, teams, and organizations utilize their God-given talents, gifts, and strengths to fulfill the specific missions they were designed to fulfill.

Know Where You're Going and Why

Our last Core leadership principle is to know where you're going and why. In other words, it's the call to fully embrace the "great days" of life. Leaders are visionaries, skilled at getting people excited about the future. But great leaders don't just know where they're going (vision); they also understand why they're going there (mission).

Having no sense of vision or mission is like taking a long road trip with no GPS. You might get somewhere, but your journey will be painful and laborious. Like you, I love the GPS feature on my smartphone. Not for one second do I miss paper maps, printing out MapQuest directions, or having to stop and ask for directions at a gas station.

Having a clear picture of where we're going and why helps leaders move forward into the unknown with confidence. To know and live our purpose, we must begin by understanding our mission, defining our values, and casting vision—for ourselves and for our teams.

Accepting Your Mission

Your mission, or purpose, provides the *why* you are on the journey towards a particular goal or destination. If someone asked you about why you exist as a person, your answer would be your personal mission. If an organization were to be asked why it exists, its representatives would answer with some type of mission statement. Any business, organization, church, parent, grandparent, spouse, or professional can—and should—have a well-defined mission.

Your mission seldom changes. It *could* change. For example, a parent moving through a life stage to become a grandparent might articulate a new and different purpose. But, for most things, the mission is constant. That is what makes it the bedrock upon which we can build. Knowing why you are here and why you exist provides foundational strength. While there may be many dreams or many visions, there is only one mission. And having a keen awareness of our mission helps control our ability to dream—and keeps us dreaming the right dreams.

Organizations and individuals sometimes spend a lot of time contemplating and writing mission statements. Often, consultants are hired. This can be money well spent, for a well-defined, simple mission statement provides quick recall of core strength.

It is also common for organizations to fall into the trap of trying to be "all things to all people" in order to sell enough products or claim a new level of stature in the marketplace. A strong understanding and commitment to one's organizational mission is critical to keep people moving toward a prioritized list of the activities necessary to achieve the mission without getting sidetracked by things that may in and of themselves be good activities but in some ways serve as a distraction from the primary mission itself.

Defining Your Values

If mission provides the context in which you live and lead, your values are parameters you choose as guideposts for decision-making. Another way to look at values is to see them as the ideals that hold an organization together and create the framework for how we do "life together" within a group or community. Values are words or phrases such as:

- Excellence in all we do
- Integrity
- Importance of all people
- Commitment to the customer
- Prompt, courteous and prepared
- Teamwork
- Servant spirit
- Truth
- Communication

Hundreds of possible values exist, so you must decide what the most significant guideposts are that will guide your decision-making. The combination of mission and values provides deep foundational strength for any individual or organization. Together, they reveal who you truly are.

We live in a world where what you do, what you have, how big you've grown, or how much you've accumulated often take center stage. Our culture is largely driven by *doing* and *having*. As a result, many lose their way—not because they lack ambition but because they haven't spent enough time considering the more important question: *Who are we?*

Who you are—and who you're becoming—is far more important than what you do or what you have. That's why mission and values are so critical to leadership. Great leaders know their mission and values, communicate them clearly, and build a culture anchored in them. They don't drift far from this foundation because they understand that mission and values are the bedrock of authentic leadership.

Casting a Vision

Humans are the only creatures who can think about the future being different from what is experienced at present and design steps to make that envisioned future come true. For instance, your dog can't sit in your yard and contemplate what life would be like if she lived with your neighbors, or in another state, or in a warmer climate. But, as people, you and I think like that constantly.

Our ability to dream and see a new future is giant and unending. A typical person can see so many possibilities in a single day. What would it be like to live in this place or that one? What would it be like to have a different job? What would it be like to make that much more money? What would it be like to be married and have a house full of children? What would it be like to win the lottery?

Leaders see the future differently from what exists today and envision steps to make that envisioned future come true. It's another of the great differences between leaders and managers. Managers control things that can be measured, so their tendency is to keep their eyes fixed on the present. They stay focused on the metrics. They assess current performance. While leaders are certainly aware of these things, they should spend much of their time lifting their eyes from the present to peer into the vast future.

Each of us should realize and utilize the gift of seeing the future. We weren't designed to stand still. We were designed to move forward.

For every worthwhile thing that exists today, someone first held a picture of it in their mind. A university, hospital, automobile, plane, space vessel, painting, business, submarine, book, computer, telephone, watch, light bulb—the list goes on. For every accomplishment of humans, the beginning was in the mind. The beginning was a picture held in the mind because God designed people in a most unusual and gifted way. He designed us to see, then create, build, accomplish, and enjoy what has been brought into reality.

What in your life did you envision in the past that is now a reality? Make a list. Your career, your spouse, your home—all of those things could be added to that list. At an earlier time in life, you dreamed of what life would be like with each of those blessings, and now what you dreamed of has become real.

Some of you reading this book are wired to see new opportunities for your teams and organizations on a regular basis. While vision, in many ways, is an unbelievably important component of leadership, it should be noted that as Uncle Ben tells his nephew Peter Parker, also known as Spider-Man, "With great power comes great responsibility."

Unregulated vision can create chaos for your team. Recently, an executive team I encountered had a running joke that they would discuss the notion of "gearing up" for every weekly team meeting because that was where they would find out the week's new list of big ideas to run after, often at the expense of the previous week's "vision."

It was a joke—sort of—but it took a terrible toll on the team's morale and sense of purpose. They became exhausted and felt as though they were chasing a new vision each week without the ability to ever catch anything. Team members described "chasing the vision" being like taking a cross-country flight with consistent turbulence, only to have the same thing happen on the return flight.

Yes, you may get to the desired destination, but it isn't something you want to do again.

Having vision without facing reality is merely hallucination. The connection between the current, realistic state of the organization and the desired future state must make sense. Should you dream big dreams? Of course! The energy derived from our dreams of the future can often be energizing and inspiring to ourselves and those we lead. But never allow your dreams to become disconnected from reality. If you do, you will also become disconnected from your team.

Another word of caution is in order at this point: Not all dreams are good for us. The mind has an enormous capacity to imagine the future, but not everything it sees is good. It can also see future evil. While some dreams come true and enhance the quality of life greatly, other dreams that come to fruition destroy not only the quality of life but also sometimes life itself.

Sorting through dreams and bringing them to reality is a process. The mind generates dreams rapidly, much like a high-speed train racing down the tracks. The train must be controlled, directed responsibly, guided along the right path, and handled with care to ensure it reaches the correct destination. Similarly, realizing a dream requires intentional control, thoughtful refinement, and strategic implementation to ensure it fulfills its true purpose and the right target is achieved. In much the same way, there is a process of controlling, handling, massaging, and implementing to bring the right dream to its right purpose.

It is not the number of pictures that race through our minds that is important; rather, it is the few we choose to hold on to. Many pictures are only fantasies or wishful thinking. They come and go quickly. The ones that come into our minds and keep returning are the ones to which we need to pay careful attention.

Research and experience testify that the pictures we hold in our minds are very significant. They affect how we act today, and those pictures tend to become reality. When we make daily decisions, sacrificial choices that are consistent with our vision will most likely become a reality. That is why all futuristic mental pictures must be built upon the foundation of mission and values. The direction we choose about the future must be consistent with who we have chosen to be (who we are) as defined by our clearly stated mission and values.

The Importance of Shared Vision

It is not enough for the leader to be the only person with a vision. The real power is when a leader can help an organization find a *shared* vision. To find and share that vision, the leader must work to develop a culture or environment that allows people to imagine all the possibilities of what *could* or *should* be for the organization.

One of my favorite leadership activities involves a simple but powerful exercise to demonstrate the importance of shared vision. A designated "leader" is given a basic sketch—perhaps a house or a star, something simple yet detailed enough to require thoughtful instruction. The rest of the group, unable to see the image, is given a random number of toothpicks and tasked with building the image based solely on the leader's verbal directions.

There are constraints to the activity: limited time, no repeated instructions, and no direct description of the image. As you might imagine, the directions often become hilariously complex: "Place one toothpick at a 90-degree angle, then another perpendicular to that, then turn it east . . ." Despite the leader's best efforts, confusion reigns. Watching the puzzled faces of participants is entertaining—but also incredibly instructive.

In all the times I've led this exercise with bright, talented "toothpick engineers," very few groups have come close to recreating the original image. The lesson is clear: Even when a leader sees the picture perfectly, others cannot follow unless they, too, have access to that same vision.

This exercise mimics the real-world challenges of leadership—limited resources, time constraints, and communication gaps that can obstruct progress. Without a shared vision, even the best teams struggle to move in the same direction.

A shared vision means everyone in the organization can see the same picture. It's not just clear and compelling—it's co-created. Even if the image is complex, if all can see it, it becomes achievable.

Organizations looking to craft strong visions for the future often benefit from reflecting on their past, recognizing their strengths, and tapping into their unrealized potential. Effective leaders listen, gathering ideas, dreams, and feedback from those around them, and then help the team answer a vital question: *What's next for us?*

Leaders must also connect the vision to real-life impact. People are far more motivated when they see how their efforts will make a difference—for their families, their colleagues, and their community. Just as important, they must feel that their personal goals align with the organization's direction.

I've facilitated many "blue sky" strategy sessions where teams come together to dream about the future. These moments reveal a lot about a group's culture and dynamics, including how open they are to possibility, the manner in which they collaborate, and their willingness to shape a new future.

But my favorite part often comes weeks or months later, when a leader calls me to share how things have shifted. Morale is up. Focus has sharpened. Engagement is stronger. Simply pausing to imagine a better future together can reignite passion and purpose.

Helping people see a new picture of what's possible is one of the greatest gifts a leader can give.

The Vision Curve

Allow me (Ken) to illustrate the concept of mission, values, and vision with a tool I've used for more than twenty-five years. I first learned about it from famed leadership guru John Maxwell.

Consider the following curve:

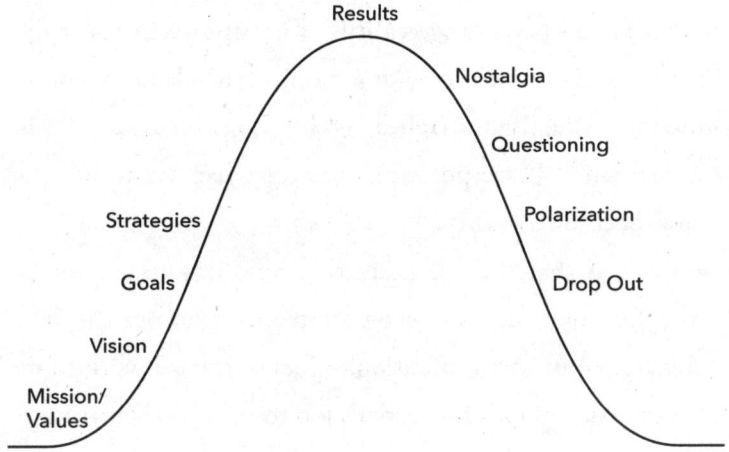

At the bottom, left-hand side, we start with *mission* and *values*. Remember, these are our foundation. Then, out of study, input, deliberation, and perhaps quietness, the crystal-clear vision is born.

Next follows a strategic plan—the pathway of how we usher in the reality we envision. Remember, humans are the only creation who can see the future differently from what it is today and take steps to make that future come true. The steps serve as the plan to achieve the vision. Moving further into the curve, at the top, we put the word *results* to signify our goal being accomplished. Our vision has been fulfilled, and we are—quite literally—living the dream.

Goals and strategies (on the left-hand side of the curve) are wonderful words to form the backbone of your strategic plan. Goals are little pieces of the vision, while strategies are action steps to meet the goal. An alternative approach is to replace these words with the concept of "obstacles to be removed." Some people are less motivated by meeting goals and more motivated by solving problems. So some leaders have learned to ask, "What stands in the way of that vision becoming reality?" This approach can galvanize certain personality types to take action. Other leaders have taken truly unconventional approaches, asking questions like: "What do we do best?" and "If we put emphasis on what we do best, would that vision become a reality?"

The point is that there is more than one way to the top of this curve. But for any vision to become a reality, you need to do *something*. You must put forth intentional, focused, hard work to make a dream come true, and it's the leader's job to refocus their team on the shared vision.

Look at the left-hand side of that curve. Isn't it exciting? Life lived on the left side of the curve is invigorating and challenging. This side of the curve is not without problems, though. Of course not! Life is full of problems. But I've found that problems encountered on the left side of the curve don't deflate so easily. Hope is still in charge, and we are moving in our purpose.

What about the right side of the curve? This side is a big part of real life for each of us. Every person, marriage, business, organization, or institution will at some point find itself on the right side—filled with frustration and discouragement.

Let's put some words on the right side and see if they sound familiar. Many different words would work—*nostalgia*, *questioning*, *polarization*, and *dropout* would all be appropriate to use. You could also say *wanting to go back*, *complaining*, *being withdrawn*, and *giving up*. However you describe it, on the right-hand side, life is not engaged, fulfilling, exciting, or fun. The more time that passes, the further down on the curve you go. The further you go, the less hope you have. And the less hope you have, the bleaker the future looks.

But here's an inspiring thought: *No one has to stay on the right side of the curve.* The way off the right side is vision, which enables you to return to the left side and then do the challenging but rewarding work of making your way back up the curve. This is where people catch the vision of a new future, become excited about a long-forgotten dream, or determine to pursue a meaningful goal. This is where we find hope for the future.

Know Where You're Going and Why

Proverbs 29:18 reminds us, "Where there is no vision, the people perish" (KJV). Vision isn't just a leadership skill—it's a lifeline. Without it, we lose direction. We drift. We settle. But with it, we awaken to possibility. We take intentional steps toward becoming who we were made to be. We endure turbulence with purpose and sacrifice with joy, and we lead with conviction.

What picture are you holding in your mind? Is it clear? Can your team repeat it back to you? Is it grounded in mission and values?

By casting vision with clarity, you may help someone experience their second "great day," the day they discover why they were born. What better way to work for the good of your people than by inviting them into the fulfilling pursuit of their life's purpose? May you lead your team, your community, or your organization into a better future than you ever imagined.

Conclusion

In my (Matt's) work with executives and corporate groups, we do an exercise where I have them envision their eightieth birthday party. I have them describe everything about it: the setting, the guest list, the energy in the room, the sights and smells and sounds.

After painting the scene, I invite them to focus on two key components: Who is there, and what stories are they telling about you? In other words, we take a moment to consider the question of influence: Who are you influencing, and how are you influencing them?

As we discussed earlier in the book, your leadership brand is made up of the stories people tell about you. All of us want to be remembered for something great, to know that our lives mattered, to believe that our presence made a difference in the world.

I've personally done this exercise many times, and now I can go into great depth and detail when describing my eightieth birthday party. I can articulate clearly where we are, what we're doing, and who is in attendance. This vision fuels me every day as I strive to cultivate the next generation of leaders.

I hope my children and future grandchildren are excited to be at my eightieth birthday party and eager to tell stories about all the adventures we had over the years and the fun memories we made together. But even more important, I hope they're telling stories about how I worked for the good and spoke up for the welfare of others. I hope they're explaining how I lived a life that wasn't focused on myself or my own ego. I hope they're describing how I had the courage to stand up and do what was right. I hope they're painting a picture of me as a man of purpose who always believed in something bigger than myself.

Now, it's your turn. Imagine with me, if you will, your eightieth birthday party. Take the time to really dig deep and contemplate the details. For some of you, it will be just a few years from now. For others, this celebration feels impossibly far away. Either way, here are some questions to consider as you reflect once more on leading from the Core:

- Are your kids or grandkids at the party? Do they want to be there, or are they being forced to attend?
- Is your spouse there, or did they choose to leave you as you climbed the corporate ladder or continued to bring your enormous ego home with you every day?
- What stories are the people in attendance sharing about you and their experiences with you?
- Is anyone you ever worked with there, and, if so, what stories are they sharing about you? Are these the stories ones you want others to hear?
- If you're uncomfortable with any of the answers to the above questions, what can you change today to start thinking more intentionally about the people in your life—the ones you have the opportunity to serve and work for?

CONCLUSION

This book was inspired by the compelling story of a teenage beauty queen and her cousin. Esther and Mordecai have lived on for thousands of years through their decision to lead from the Core. Esther's courage prevented a genocide. Mordecai's commitment to work for the good of the people and speak for their welfare shaped the course of the ancient world.

Your commitment to the leadership Core will leave behind a story that others will tell, the same way I told you the story of Esther and Mordecai, the same way people stood at Dr. Jackson's retirement dinner and told stories about him.

May you enjoy a lifetime of "great days" as you lead from the Core, and may each of you live a good story—one worth telling.

Work for the good of the people.
Keep your ego in check.
Embrace truth.
Lead with your ears.
Show up with grace.
Pace yourself and extend the game.
Be coachable.
Know where you're going and why.

ACKNOWLEDGEMENTS

Throughout the spring and summer of 2024, I called Dr. Ken Jones multiple times to discuss the pull I felt to start a leadership development consulting firm to help values-driven organizations focus on the growth and development of their people and teams. I remember telling him that I wanted to start a company that was designed to "work for the good of the people who were trying to work for the good of the people." I will never forget the moment when he said to me, "Matt, you are going to need a book to legitimize yourself in the leadership consulting market, and I think I have some things that might help you get started. Why don't we write it together?"

What Dr. Jones didn't know at the time was that I had a sticky note on my laptop that said, "Beg, borrow, buy, or steal some of the core principles from Dr. Jones for a book."

I remember the hair on my arms standing up. For the man who first introduced me to the study of leadership as a student and then as a young professional to offer to write a book with me on the topic without knowing it was already on my mind was an incredible moment.

His principles had helped frame my own approach to leadership, and when added to some of the principles I had developed on my own over the years, I knew we could put together something practical yet powerful for people to have something strong to stand on as they seek to lead and make a difference in the world.

I cannot say thank you enough to Dr. Jones for his mentorship, the fire he lit in me for the study of leadership all those years ago, and also for blessing me with the opportunity to take this book idea and run with it. You live these principles every day, and I am eternally grateful for the example you have been to me and so many others. It is a true honor to be your co-author.

What I didn't fully understand at the onset was just how many people it would take to put together the Core. There are so many people who have helped from the moment we decided to jump into this project.

There are not enough words to explain just how grateful I am for Scott Smith and Stan Lowery, my business partners at Great Days Leadership. Your belief in me, this book, and in the work I get to do each day to help develop leaders has been instrumental in all of this becoming a reality.

To Rachel Miller and Charlie Sells, your gifts with words and your insights helped shape so much of how the world will encounter this book. Your belief in the book's message has been such a blessing along the way.

To Dr. John Delony, your friendship and offer to be a part of this book are something that I will never forget.

To Greg Brown, Dr. Kathy Crockett, Elizabeth Cole, Dr. Rachel Goode, Tom Heinselman, Mckenzie Masters, and Clint Rhodes, I appreciate so much your friendship and willingness to read early drafts of this book. The value of the feedback you provided was immeasurable.

To Justin Batt, Jill Smith, Landon Dickerson, and the entire team at Forefront Books, thank you so much for your professionalism and attention to detail. Dr. Jones and I appreciate all you have done to move this book across the finish line. We are looking forward to the next one!

To John Mason and Daniel Hope, the literal spaces you provided in your office and in your cabin provided me the calm and quiet places I needed to think creatively and bring these ideas to life.

To our family members, we love you and are so grateful for the care and interest you have shown us as we worked through this material.

To each of our colleagues, clients, friends, and co-laborers, we say thank you for your encouragement and thoughtfulness as we talked through these concepts with you.

Above all, I must declare my thanks to our Lord and Savior, Jesus Christ, for your love, mercy, and grace, and for serving as the ultimate leadership example.

In Him,
Matt Paden

ABOUT THE AUTHORS

Dr. Matt Paden is the president and managing partner of Great Days Leadership, where he helps leaders and organizations grow with purpose, integrity, and impact. With more than two decades of experience as an executive, consultant, speaker, and coach, Matt specializes in aligning teams around mission, building healthy cultures, and developing clear, values-driven leadership. Holding a doctorate in organizational leadership from Pepperdine University, Matt brings a principled yet practical approach to developing leaders and driving organizational change. His work centers on igniting purpose, service, faith, and developing leadership in others, empowering them to create lasting influence in their workplaces and communities. He lives in Franklin, Tennessee, with his wife and their two children.

Dr. L. Ken Jones was appointed president of Oklahoma Christian University (OC) on May 1, 2023. He and his wife, Suzie, are natives of Cordell, Oklahoma, where they currently have involvement in farming and ranching. Dr. Jones was educated in the field of engineering receiving his PhD from Oklahoma State University. His career spans engineering, pulpit preaching, leadership training, and higher education leadership. Dr. Jones served as president of Lubbock

ABOUT THE AUTHORS

Christian University (LCU) for nineteen years and chancellor for five years. He has spent over four decades in Christian higher education and leadership training. Ken and Suzie have two grown married children, and four grandchildren. For years, he has been a frequent speaker in churches, corporations, and other groups.